THE FOREST FOR THE TREES?
Government Policies and the Misuse of Forest Resources

Robert Repetto

WORLD RESOURCES INSTITUTE
A Center for Policy Research

May 1988

Kathleen Courrier
Publications Director

Don Strandberg
Marketing Manager

Hyacinth Billings
Production Supervisor

FAO Photo
Cover

Each World Resources Institute Report represents a timely, scientific treatment of a subject of public concern. WRI takes responsibility for choosing the study topics and guaranteeing its authors and researchers freedom of inquiry. It also solicits and responds to the guidance of advisory panels and expert reviewers. Unless otherwise stated, however, all the interpretation and findings set forth in WRI publications are those of the authors.

Contents

Acknowledgments

We wish to thank the authors of country case studies, whose scholarly insights contributed so much to the study, and thank as well as the many others who assisted in the research—Tinling Choong, Mark Dillenbeck, Ruth Griswold, Philip Huffman, Nancy Sheehan and Craig Thomas. Hyacinth Billings, Esther Chambers, Katherine Harrington and Karen Saxon put forth dedicated efforts in the lengthy production process.

We also wish to acknowledge the useful contributions and comments received from Paul Aird, Michael Arnold, Peter Ashton, Peter Emerson, Julian Evans, Suzannah Hecht, Carl Gallegos, Barin Ganguli, Alan Grainger, Hans Gregersen, Roberto Lopez C., Norman Myers, Jeffrey Sayer, John Spears, William Beattie and Roger Sedjo. We appreciate the support of WRI's advisory panel on the study of economic incentives for sustainable development: William Baumol of New York University, Gardner Brown Jr. at the University of Washington, Anthony Fisher at the University of California at Berkeley, Shanta Devarajan at Harvard, Charles Howe at the University of Colorado, and Jeremy Warford at the World Bank. Colleagues at WRI, including Kathleen Courrier, Peter Hazlewood, Jessica Mathews and Gus Speth, provided strong support.

R.R.

Contributors

Eufresina L. Boado, (Ph.D. Forest Resources Management, State University of New York at Syracuse) was formerly the Executive Officer, Project Management Staff, Philippine Forestry Bureau, Manila, Philippines and was the Project Coordinator, ASEAN, Manila, Philippines

John Browder, Visiting Assistant Professor of Planning and Geography, Center for Latin American Studies, Tulane University, New Orleans, Louisiana

Kong Fanwen, Research Fellow, Institute of Forestry Economics, Chinese Academy of Forestry Sciences, Beijing

Malcolm Gillis, Dean of Graduate Schools, Vice-Provost for Academic Affairs, and Professor of Public Policy and Economics, Duke University, Durham, North Carolina

Li Jinchang, Director, Technical Economics Section, Research Center for Economic, Technological, and Social Development under the State Council of the People's Republic of China, Beijing

He Naihui, Deputy Chief Editor, Linye Jingji (Forestry Economics), Institute of Forestry Economics, Chinese Academy of Forestry Sciences, Beijing

Robert Repetto, Director, Program in Economics and Institutions, World Resources Institute, Washington, D.C.

Lester Ross, (Ph.D. Political Science, University of Michigan) is a J.D. Candidate at the Harvard Law School, Cambridge, Massachusetts

Foreword

Throughout much of the Third World, accelerating deforestation is laying waste to vital economic assets, destroying fragile soils, and driving wild species to extinction. In industrialized countries as well, forests are imperilled by pollution and contested by conflicting uses. Warnings have reached us, both from satellite images that show forests in remote areas now much smaller than reported in official statistics, and from desperate forest dwellers protecting with their lives their diminishing legacy. Scientists have drawn for us the connections between deforestation and genetic impoverishment, economic deprivation, and climate change.

What can be done to protect and use these resources more wisely? Many have attributed the loss of forests in the Third World to relentless pressures from growing populations, land-hungry small farmers, and rural households in search of fuelwood and forage. These pressures are real, but a different and powerful force is often overlooked.

In many countries, government policies lie behind the wastage of forest resources. Tax incentives and credit subsidies guarantee large profits to private investors who convert forests to pastures and farms, whether or not these competing uses are sustainable. Governments allow private concessionaires to log the national forests on terms that induce uneconomic or wasteful uses of the public domain. Massive public expenditures on highways, dams, plan-

tations, and agricultural settlements, too often supported by multilateral development lending, convert or destroy large areas of forest for projects of questionable economic worth.

Robert Repetto, Director of WRI's economic research program, and an international group of seven collaborators, including researchers in China, Brazil, and the Philippines have documented these policies and the ensuing ecological and economic losses. *The Forest for the Trees? Government Policies and the Misuse of Forest Resources*, the first full report of their findings, examines the situation in ten countries on four continents. It shows that instead of an inexorable conflict between economic development and forest conservation, there are ready opportunities to promote both by improving current government policies.

Consider just a few of the findings:

- Between 1979 and 1982, Indonesia's government sacrificed over $2 billion dollars of potential forest revenues to logging concessionaires and allied interests, fueling a destructive timber boom.

- In the Philippines, over these same years, forced forest-based industrialization gave rise to inefficient mills that lost $500 million in potential resource rents.

- Generous tax and credit incentives created over 12 million hectares of large cattle ranches in the Brazilian Amazon, even though the typical ranch could cover less than half its costs without these subsidies.

- On more than 100 million acres of national forests, the U.S. Forest Service consistently produces and sells timber that isn't worth the direct cost of harvesting and marketing it, sacrificing potential recreational and wildlife benefits.

Painful facts like these and others are found in *The Forest for the Trees? Government Policies and the Misuse of Forest Resources* and the much longer book that will present the full country case studies (*Public Policy and the Misuse of Forest Resources*, Cambridge University Press, fall 1988). They have far-reaching policy implications. Indeed, they shift the debate over how to manage forest resources for development. No longer can governments justify forest destruction as the unfortunate but necessary road to economic development. If the policies that have sacrificed so much of the world's forest estate are themselves costly and the alternative uses they promote are often uneconomic, then creating a better policy framework is the first step toward sustainable resource management.

The policy recommendations spelled out in *The Forest for the Trees? Government Policies and the Misuse of Forest Resources* complement those implicit in *Tropical Forests: A Call for Action* (The World Resources Institute, The World Bank, and the United Nations Development Programme, 1985), which identified the need for increased attention to and investment in the forest sector. Policy reform and increased development effort go hand in hand. Unless policies that induce forest destruction are changed, investments in reforestation, watershed management, and wildlife conservation will be overwhelmed.

This report also extends the findings in Robert Repetto's recent WRI studies on the harmful effects of large government subsidies to pesticide sales and irrigation projects (*Paying the Price: Pesticide Subsidies in the Developing Countries* and *Skimming the Water: Rent-Seeking and the Performance of Public Irrigation Systems*). In these and related studies, WRI has committed itself to finding and publicizing practical policies that promote more sustainable use of the global resource base.

Financial support for this study was provided by the United States Agency for International Development, the World Bank, and the World Commission for Environment and Development. WRI's overall program on tropical forests has received support from the W. Alton Jones Foundation, the Andrew W. Mellon Foundation, the Jessie Smith Noyes Foundation, the David and Lucile Packard Foundation, and the Pew Charitable Trusts. To all these institutions, we express our deep appreciation.

James Gustave Speth
President
World Resources Institute

I. Overview

Threats to the world's forests are evoking responses at all levels, from villagers organizing to protect their woods to international summit meetings of world leaders. Experts have clearly established the extent of forest decline and likely economic, social, and environmental consequences.* They have also discussed deforestation's principal causes: three symptoms of population growth and rural poverty—shifting cultivation, agricultural conversion, and fuelwood gathering—that threaten natural forests in the Third World. Commercial exploitation, including logging and land-clearing for ranches and agricultural estates, have also been identified as sources of large forest losses.

This report goes further by showing how governments, committed in principle to conservation and wise resource use, are aggravating the losses of the forests under their stewardship through mistaken policies. Such policies, by and large, were adopted for worthy objectives: industrial or agricultural growth, regional development, job creation, or poverty alleviation. But, this study finds such objectives typically have not been realized or have been attained only at excessive cost.

*Brown 1985; Eckholm 1976; Fearnside 1982; Grainger 1980; Lanly 1982; Myers 1980, 1984, 1985; Spears 1979, Allen and Barnes 1985; Bunker 1980; Ehrlich and Ehrlich 1981; Plumwood and Routley 1982; Tucker and Richards 1983.

Throughout the world, governments largely determine how forests should be used. In the industrialized countries, a substantial percentage of remaining forests are on public lands. According to a comprehensive FAO assessment, in the Third World over 80 percent of the closed forest area are public lands. (Lanly 1982.) Governments have taken over authority and responsibility for managing them from indigenous communities, which traditionally used the forests in accordance with their own laws.

Governments committed in principle to conservation and wise resource use, are aggravating the losses of the forests under their stewardship through mistaken policies.

Even the use of private forests is greatly influenced by government policies, whether intentionally or not. Because commercial forestry involves holding a growing asset for long periods, returns to private investors are sensitive to credit costs, inflation, taxes on land and capital assets, and other economic parameters greatly affected by government policy. Because some forest lands can be used for agricultural or other purposes, government policies that stimulate expansion of these competing land uses can do so at the expense of forest area.

1

> *Land areas should be devoted to the uses, forest or non-forest, that yield the greatest potential economic benefits—whether or not those benefits are reflected in market transactions.*

One widely accepted economic criterion for forest management is getting the maximum total benefit from all the forests' various possible uses over the long run, discounting future benefits at an appropriate interest rate. This is a criterion for economic efficiency in forest use. It implies that land areas should be devoted to the uses, forest or non-forest, that yield the greatest potential economic benefits—whether or not those benefits are reflected in market transactions. For example, applying the efficiency criterion means that land most valuable as a watershed protection forest would not be converted to crops; a forest most valuable as a recreational park would not be clear-cut for timber; or, a forest containing immense mineral reserves would not be preserved as wilderness.

In countries endowed with large forest resources, government policies frequently violate this criterion for efficient resource use, resulting in economic and fiscal losses while contributing to the wastage of forest resources. In the United States, for example, many of the national forests have been managed primarily for timber production of marginal or even negative economic value, at the expense of other potential uses. Wasteful use in this economic sense does not ignore or minimize the importance of non-economic objectives underlying forest policies. Rather, policies leading to economic waste have also undermined conservation, regional development strategies, and other socio-economic goals.

Forestry policies, the terms on which potential users can exploit public forests, include harvesting fees, royalties, logging regulations,

and administration of timber concessions with private loggers. Governments have typically sold off timber too cheaply, sacrificing public revenues and the undervalued non-timber benefits of the standing forest while encouraging "timber booms," profiteering, and rapid logging exploitation. Also, the terms of many timber concession agreements and revenue systems have encouraged excessive "high-grading" of the forests and wasteful, resource-depleting logging.

Other government policies impinging significantly on the forest sector include tax and trade regimes, industrialization incentives, land tenure laws, and agricultural resettlement programs. These frequently are strongly biased against forest preservation and toward their

> *Policies leading to economic waste have also undermined conservation, regional development strategies, and other socio-economic goals.*

exploitation or conversion to other land uses. They thus tip the balance of incentives facing private parties to exploit or convert forest resources far faster and further than market forces would otherwise allow. In several countries studied, such biases have been strong enough to destroy forest resources for purposes that are intrinsically uneconomic.

Many Third World Governments have become more aware in recent years of the threats and risks of forest depletion. Most have reacted by adopting new measures to encourage reforestation, but few have modified existing policies that have aggravated forest depletion. As a result, in all the developing countries studied, deforestation continues at significant rates.

While increased attention, investment, and research directed toward solving forest problems are now widely advocated, the special contribution of this report and the underlying research is in identifying the government policies that can be changed to reduce forest wastage without sacrificing other economic objectives and that must be changed to ensure that other interventions will be effective.

The case studies in this study give examples of these policy opportunities. Country investigations undertaken in China, Indonesia, three separate regions of Malaysia, the Philippines, Brazil, Ghana, Liberia, the Ivory Coast, Gabon, and the United States were carried out either by local analysts and research institutions or by U.S. researchers with long-term local interests and experience. These countries represent dif-

---

Which government policies can be changed to reduce forest wastage without sacrificing other economic objectives and which must be changed to ensure that other interventions will be effective?

---

ferent continents, different economic systems, different levels of development, and different ecological zones. The settings, the problems, and the opportunities differ among them. Yet, there are also surprising similarities.

The Extent and Rate of Deforestation

Scientific evidence suggests that the world's forest area has declined by one-fifth, from about 5 to 4 billion hectares, from pre-agricultural times to the present. Temperate closed forests have suffered the greatest losses (32 to 35 percent), followed by subtropical woody savannahs and deciduous forests (24 to 25 percent), and tropical climax forests (15 to 20 percent). Over the entire period, tropical evergreen rainforests have suffered the smallest

attrition, 4 to 6 percent, because until recently they were inaccessible and barely populated. (Matthews 1983.) Forests and woods still cover two fifths of the earth's land surface *(Table I.1),* three and a half times the area devoted to crops, and account for about 60 percent of the net biomass productivity of terrestrial ecosystems. (Olson 1975.) Just over half of the remaining forests are in the developing countries.

Since World War II, deforestation has shifted to the tropics. In the richer temperate zones, rural outmigration and rising agricultural yields have allowed abandoned farms to revert to woods. Forest management still poses acute policy issues, as industrialists, loggers, naturalists, hikers and hunters urge their conflicting interests, but the forest area is stable.

In the developing countries, the issues are more intense, because for hundreds of millions, the struggle is for survival. Growing rural populations invade the forests in search of land for their crops, fuel for cooking, and fodder for their animals. Governments impelled to raise foreign exchange earnings and employment, and to finance economic development programs, turn to the forests as a readily exploitable resource. Under this relentless assault, Third World forests are retreating. Yearly, more than 11 million hectares are cleared for other uses—7.5 and 3.8 million hectares of closed and open forests respectively— and in most developing countries, deforestation is accelerating. Between 1950 and 1983, forest and woodland areas dropped 38 percent in Central America and 24 percent in Africa. *(See Table I.2.)* Recent remote sensing data from several countries suggest that even these figures, based on FAO statistics, may be considerably underestimated. At current deforestation rates, forests in Nigeria, Ivory Coast, Paraguay, Costa Rica, Haiti, and El Salvador, which are already much diminished, would disappear within 30 years. Other countries, especially Indonesia, Brazil, and Colombia, have large reserves but are losing vast areas every year.

Table I.1. Land Use 1850–1980 (million hectares)

	1850	1900	1950	1980
Ten Regions				
Forests and Woodlands	5,919	5,749	5,345	5,007
Grassland and Pasture	6,350	6,284	6,293	6,299
Croplands	538	773	1,169	1,501
Tropical Africa				
Forests and Woodlands	1,336	1,306	1,188	1,074
Grassland and Pasture	1,061	1,075	1,130	1,158
Croplands	57	73	136	222
North Africa and Middle East				
Forests and Woodlands	34	30	18	14
Grassland and Pasture	1,119	1,115	1,097	1,060
Croplands	27	37	66	107
North America				
Forests and Woodlands	971	954	939	942
Grassland and Pasture	571	504	446	447
Croplands	50	113	206	203
Latin America				
Forests and Woodlands	1,420	1,394	1,273	1,151
Grassland and Pasture	621	634	700	767
Croplands	18	33	87	142
China				
Forests and Woodlands	96	84	69	58
Grassland and Pasture	799	797	793	778
Croplands	75	89	108	134
South Asia				
Forests and Woodlands	317	299	251	180
Grassland and Pasture	189	189	190	187
Croplands	71	89	136	210
Southeast Asia				
Forests and Woodlands	252	249	242	235
Grassland and Pasture	123	118	105	92
Croplands	7	15	35	55
Europe				
Forests and Woodlands	160	156	154	167
Grassland and Pasture	150	142	136	138
Croplands	132	145	152	137

Table I.1. Continued

	1850	1900	1950	1980
USSR				
Forests and Woodlands	1,067	1,014	952	941
Grassland and Pasture	1,078	1,078	1,070	1,065
Croplands	94	147	216	233
Pacific Developed Countries				
Forests and Woodlands	267	263	258	246
Grassland and Pasture	638	634	625	608
Croplands	6	14	28	58

Source: World Resources Report 1987: 272

Large as they are, these figures show only the area completely cleared for other uses. But, forests and woodlands are also deteriorating in quality. Each year over 4 million hectares of virgin tropical forests are harvested, becoming ''secondary'' forest. (Melillo et al. 1985.) Under prevailing practices, most of the mature stems of those few species with commercial value are removed (usually amounting to 10 to 20 percent of standing volume) but typically another 30 to 50 percent of the trees are destroyed or fatally damaged during logging and the soil is sufficiently disturbed to impede regeneration, even in the long run. (Guppy 1984.)

In the open woodlands and savannahs of drier regions, where plant growth is slower, fuelwood and fodder demands are outstripping regeneration as populations grow and tree stocks diminish. In Africa's Sahelian/Sudanian zone, for example, consumption now exceeds natural regeneration by 70 percent in Sudan, 75 percent in northern Nigeria, 150 percent in Ethiopia, and 200 percent in Niger. (Anderson and Fishwick 1984.) Worldwide, the FAO estimates that 1.5 of the 2 billion people who rely mostly on wood fuel are cutting wood faster than it is growing back. (FAO 1983.) Woodlands become progressively sparser and eventually disappear under such pressures.

Simple projections based on the growth of population and food demands, and inversely on the increase in agricultural yields, predict a declining deforestation rate that would reduce the tropical forest area by 10 to 20 percent by 2020. *(See Table I.3.)* The projected deceleration reflects assumed declining population growth rates and the slowing of growth in food demand relative to that of per capita income. However, feedbacks between logging and shifting cultivation, migration of farmers into forest areas, and cash crop demands could easily produce much higher deforestation rates than those projected. (Grainger 1987.)

The outlook for tropical timber is also unfavorable. Demand is not limited to subsistence needs in the developing countries but springs largely from rapidly growing demands in richer countries of the North for exotic tropical hardwoods. *(See Table 1.4.)*

Future timber harvests and exports are predicted to decline dramatically due to depletion of commercial stands. According to the recent report of an international task force convened by the World Resources Institute, the World Bank, and the United Nations Development Programme, ''By the end of the century, the 33 developing countries that are now net

Table I.2. Deforestation in Tropical Countries 1981–85

Country	Closed Forest Area 1980 (thousand hectares)	Annual Rate of Deforestation 1981–85 (percent)	Area Deforested Annually (thousand hectares)
GROUP I[a]			
Colombia	46,400	1.8	820
Mexico	46,250	1.0	470
Ecuador	14,250	2.4	340
Paraguay	4,070	4.7	190
Nicaragua	4,496	2.3	105
Guatemala	4,442	1.6	72
Costa Rica	1,638	4.0	65
Honduras	3,797	1.3	48
Panama	4,165	0.9	36
Malaysia	20,996	1.2	255
Thailand	9,235	2.6	244
Lao People's Dem Rep	8,410	1.2	100
Philippines	9,510	1.0	91
Nepal	1,941	4.1	80
Vietnam	8,770	0.7	60
Sri Lanka	1,659	3.5	58
Nigeria	5,950	5.0	300
Ivory Coast	4,458	6.5	290
Madagascar	10,300	1.2	128
Liberia	2,000	2.1	42
Guinea	2,050	1.8	36
Angola	2,900	1.2	34
Zambia	3,010	1.0	30
Ghana	1,718	1.3	22
Total	**222,415**	**2.3**	**3,916**
GROUP II[b]			
Brazil	357,480	0.4	1,360
Peru	69,680	0.4	260
Venezuela	31,870	0.4	125
Bolivia	44,010	0.2	87
Indonesia	113,895	0.5	600
Zaire	105,750	0.2	160
India	51,841	0.3	132
Burma	31,941	0.3	102
Cameroon	17,920	0.4	80
Kampuchea, Dem	7,548	0.3	25
Papua New Guinea	34,230	0.1	22
Congo	21,340	0.1	22
Gabon	20,500	0.1	15
Total	**908,005**	**0.3**	**2,990**

Table I.2. Continued

Country	Closed Forest Area 1980 (thousand hectares)	Annual Rate of Deforestation 1981–85 (percent)	Area Deforested Annually (thousand hectares)
GROUP III[c]			
El Salvador	141	2.8	4
Jamaica	67	3.0	2
Haiti	48	1.2	1
Guinea-Bissau	660	2.6	17
Kenya	1,105	1.0	11
Mozambique	935	1.1	10
Uganda	765	1.3	10
Brunei[e]	325	2.2	7
Rwanda	120	2.3	3
Benin	47	2.6	1
Total	**6,529**	**2.2**	**66**
GROUP IV[d]			
Belize[e]	1,385	0.6	9
Dominican Republic	629	0.4	2
Cuba	1,455	0.1	2
Trinidad and Tobago	208	0.4	1
Bangladesh	927	0.9	8
Pakistan	2,185	0.0	1
Bhutan	2,100	0.0	1
Tanzania	1,440	0.7	10
Ethiopia	4,350	0.1	6
Sierra Leone	740	0.8	6
Central African Rep	3,590	0.1	5
Sudan	650	0.6	4
Somalia	1,540	0.2	3
Equatorial Guinea	1,295	0.2	3
Togo	304	0.7	2
Total	**23,458**	**0.4**	**80**

Notes:
a. higher than average rates of deforestation and large areas affected
b. relatively low rates but large areas affected
c. high rates and small areas of forests remaining
d. low or moderate rates and small areas affected
e. source: World Resources Report 1986

Source: World Resources Report 1987

Table I.3. Projected High and Low Deforestation Rates 1980–2020

		High Scenario					Low Scenario				
		1980	1990	2000	2010	2020	1980	1990	2000	2010	2020
Deforestation Rates (ha.106.a-1)											
Africa	(1.1)	1.6	1.5	1.2	0.9	0.9	1.0	0.9	0.7	0.6	0.4
Asia-Pacific	(1.3)	1.7	1.5	1.2	1.2	1.1	1.1	0.9	0.7	0.5	0.4
Latin America	(3.1)	3.3	3.1	2.7	2.2	1.7	2.0	1.6	1.1	0.6	0.0
Humid Tropics	(5.6)	6.6	6.1	5.1	4.3	3.7	4.1	3.4	2.5	1.7	0.9
Forest Area (ha.106)											
Africa		198.9	183.5	170.3	160.4	151.6	198.9	188.9	181.1	175.0	170.1
Asia-Pacific		239.4	222.8	209.5	197.5	185.8	239.4	228.9	220.8	214.8	210.2
Latin America		598.0	566.2	537.5	513.0	493.8	598.0	580.1	566.7	558.6	555.8
Humid Tropics		1036.3	972.6	917.2	870.8	831.1	1036.3	997.9	968.7	948.5	936.1

*(Lanly estimates for 1976–80 in brackets)

Source: Grainger 1987

Demand for tropical timber is not limited to subsistence needs in the developing countries but springs largely from rapidly growing demands in richer countries of the North for exotic tropical hardwoods.

exporters of forest products will be reduced to fewer than 10, and total developing-country exports of industrial forest products are predicted to drop from their current level of more than US$7 billion to less than US$2 billion.'' (World Resources Institute 1985.) Depletion is becoming evident in Asia, where once-leading exporters like the Philippines have already virtually exhausted their lowland productive forests. But, Africa, and Latin America are seen as able to fill the market only for another few decades before thinning of their commercial stands also raises supply

costs. *(See Table I.5. and Figure I.1.)* (Grainger 1987.) Although some losses in foreign exchange earnings will probably be offset by rising timber prices and increased value added from domestic processing, severe depletion of an extremely valuable natural resource within a single generation is the forecast.

Tropical forests are slow to recover fully once disturbed; and, although total primary productivity is high, the annual growth of the rela-

Although some losses in foreign exchange earnings will probably be offset by rising timber prices and increased value added from domestic processing, severe depletion of an extremely valuable natural resource within a single generation is the forecast.

Table 1.4. International Trade in Forest Products

Trade in Sawlogs & Veneer-Logs, Sawnwood and Wood-Based Panels (000m³)	1961	1970 (1961–1970)	1979 (1970–1979)	1985 (1979–1985)
I. Exports, World Total (annual average growth rates)	65437	130312 (8%)	177706 (3%)	167653 (−1%)
Developing Market Economics, Total	16696	44644 (11%)	59963 (3%)	44155 (−5%)
Africa, Total	5551	8128 (4%)	7427 (−1%)	5238 (−6%)
Latin America, Total	2148	2661 (2%)	4352 (6%)	3935 (−2%)
Asia, Total	8971	33381 (16%)	47393 (4%)	33444 (−6%)
II. Imports, World Total	64750	126508 (8%)	178150 (4%)	167524 (−1%)
Developed Market Economics, Total	56343	107505 (7%)	142133 (3%)	127387 (−2%)
North America	12791	19880 (5%)	34707 (6%)	43332 (4%)
West Europe	32292	43839 (3%)	56638 (3%)	48080 (−3%)
Asia	10021	42658 (17%)	49685 (2%)	34433 (−6%)
Developing Economics, Total	4808	11704 (10%)	23526 (8%)	21629 (−1%)

Source: FAO, *Forest Production Yearbook,* various years

tively few prized commercial species is relatively low in a heterogeneous stand. Although secondary tree species will quickly revegetate forest clearings unless soils have been severely depleted, canopy trees and large individuals emerging through the canopy may take a hundred years or more to mature, and the density of commercial stems will likely be lower than in the original stand. (Richards 1973.) Moreover, there is little experience with felling and silvicultural systems able to maintain harvest values through several successive harvests. (Mergen and Vincent 1987.)

Some economists have therefore examined whether sustained yield management can be justified on strict investment principles, especially since high transport costs and limited market demand for little-known varieties greatly reduces the stumpage value of residual

Table I.5. Projected Exports of Logs and Processed Wood from Developing Countries 1980–2020

Trends in Exports (m3.106)

	1980	1985	1990	1995	2000	2005	2010	2015	2020
AFRICA									
Base	7.9	7.7	11.4	15.8	32.8	33.7	21.6	25.2	8.1
High	7.9	7.0	12.1	20.4	57.2	22.0	15.3	5.7	6.0
ASIA-PACIFIC									
Base	41.5	47.3	35.6	30.9	12.1	13.3	11.8	4.2	7.1
High	41.5	50.0	28.5	28.4	15.0	4.2	7.0	4.5	5.4
LATIN AMERICA									
Base	1.2	8.4	32.2	51.7	77.0	104.0	55.4	33.2	20.7
High	1.2	9.5	46.3	63.9	73.2	64.5	33.9	10.8	4.0

Source: Grainger 1987

species. (Leslie 1987.) The alternative is to harvest these mature forests and convert the land to higher-yielding plantations, ranches, or farms.

This alternative omits important arguments for sustained use management. First, tropical forests as a standing resource confer important ongoing benefits that improve conservation's economic return. (Hartman 1976.) For the 500 million forest dwellers worldwide, a wide variety of nuts, berries, game, fish, honey, and other foodstuffs are available. The value of these yields are badly underestimated, since they hardly ever register as market transactions and benefit mostly weak cultural minorities. But resins, essential oils, medicinal substances, rattan, flowers, and a wide variety of other products flow into commercial channels. Although they are generally regarded as "minor" forest products and receive little promotion or development attention, their aggregate value is substantial. Exports of such products from Indonesia, for example, reached US$125 million per year by the early 1980s, most of which represented employment income for those engaged in collection and trade.

These products are a small fraction of the potential sustainable yield of the tropical forests, which springs from their astounding biological diversity, only a tiny fraction of which has been investigated. (Myers, 1984) Ecuador, with a land area only 3 percent as large as Europe's, shelters 20 to 50 percent more plant species. A single hectare of tropical forest may contain 300 different trees, most of them represented by a single individual. The Amazon contains one fifth of all bird species on earth, and at least eight times as many fish species as the Mississippi River system. (U.S. Congress, Office of Technology Assessment 1987.)

Tropical forests contribute genetic materials that plant breeders can use to confer disease and pest resistance upon coffee, cocoa, bananas and pineapples, maize, rice and many other crops. They contribute entirely new foods such as the mangosteen and the winged bean. Pyrethrins, rotenoids, and other insecticides have evolved in tropical plants in self-defense, while insect predators and parasites found in tropical forests control at least 250 different agricultural pests. (Myers 1984.) Tropical plants

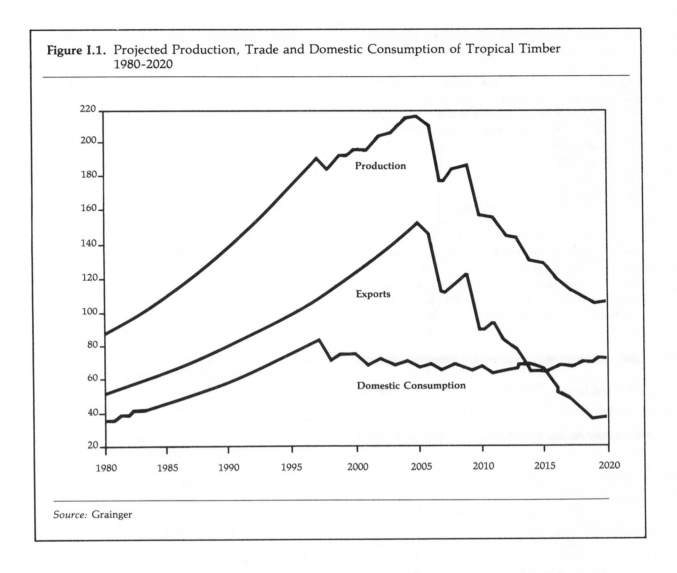

Figure I.1. Projected Production, Trade and Domestic Consumption of Tropical Timber 1980-2020

Source: Grainger

underlie one-quarter of all prescription drugs sold in the United States. (U.S. Congress, Office of Technology Assessment 1987.) Alkaloids such as quinine, reserpine (used in drugs to control hypertension) and vincristine (vital in treating childhood leukemia and Hodgkin's disease); plant steroids such as diosgenin, which comes from Mexican yams and is used in oral contraceptives, are some of the pharmaceutical products from tropical plants.

Current uses represent only a very minor fraction of the potential benefits. While a score or so of plants make up the large bulk of the human diet, 10,000 foods from plants and animals are known, mainly in the tropics. Forest-dwelling Indians in the Amazon know of 1,300 medicinal plants, including antibiotics, narcotics, abortifacients, contraceptives, antidiarrheal agents, fungicides, anaesthetics, muscle relaxants and many others, most of which have never been investigated by Western scientists. The sacrifice of these current and potential benefits as the tropics are deforested and endemic species (and indigenous knowledge of them) are lost is generally omitted from economic analyses of forest management options.

Second, the yields of alternative land uses have been greatly overestimated. The soils underlying 95 percent of the remaining tropical forests are infertile and easily degraded through erosion, laterization, or other processes if the vegetative cover is removed. Unlike temperate regions, where organic matter can build up in the soil, high temperatures and rainfall quickly deplete nutrients in the soil, so that most of the entire nutrient stock is in the biomass itself, where it is quickly and efficiently recycled. (Breunig 1985.) The tropical forest ecosystem is highly adapted, to the extent that dense forests can even exist on what is essentially sand. Attempts to substitute monocultures typically encounter declining yields and invasion by pest and weed species.

The yields of alternative land uses have been greatly overestimated.

(National Research Council 1982.) Plantation crops that are most successful in the tropics are those such as tea, cocoa and rubber that remove relatively little of the nutrient stock. Traditional long-fallow shifting cultivation systems also give the forest ecosystem ample time to recover, but most annual cropping efforts have proved to be economic as well as ecological failures. Agricultural settlement schemes and large-scale plantations have incurred economic losses, and, if not covered by continuing government subsidies, have led to the eventual abandonment of large areas of degraded soils and impoverished biota. (Buschbacher, Uhl, and Serrao 1987.) These losses are rarely entered into the calculus of expected benefits and costs. Instead, as this report shows, some governments provide generous incentives to encourage conversion in the illusory expectation of higher returns, and then absorb the ensuing losses.

Finally, the economic benefits from timber harvests to the national economies of tropical countries are substantially overstated. The gross value of timber exports is the usual focus of attention. Overlooked are the large acknowledged and hidden outflows of profits gained by domestic and foreign timber concessionaires and the politicians and military officers who are often their silent partners. The net domestic benefits gained by the economies of tropical countries from depletion of their forest resources have been surprisingly small, as several of the following case studies document. Value-added in the forestry sector averaged 3.3 percent of GDP in a 1980 sample of African countries, and this low figure substantially overstates its contribution to income: a substantial fraction of value-added should be regarded as depreciation of the forest sector's capital stock rather than as current income. (Repetto et al. 1987.) In some countries, including the Philippines, annual revenues accruing to national treasuries from forest exploitation have not covered even the administrative and infrastructure costs incurred for timber harvesting. The same is true in dozens of the national forests of the United States, where forestry policy and practice are usually presumed to be more developed. On balance, the narrow economic case for "mining" tropical forests as an exhaustible resource is far from established, and there is no justification for exploiting the resource as wastefully and destructively as many countries have done. In fact, economic and ecological losses have gone hand in hand.

The Reasons for Deforestation in Tropical Countries

The reasons for the rapid deforestation taking place in the Third World are complex. Some are rooted deeply in countries' development patterns: rapidly increasing populations, extreme concentration of landholdings that leave hundreds of millions in search of land, slow growth of job opportunities in both city and countryside. The Ivory Coast, where immigration and natural increase produced population growth at 4.6 percent per year between 1965 and 1985 (by far the most rapid in the world), also experienced accelerating deforestation, from an annual rate of 2.4 percent per year between 1956 and 1965 to one of 7.3 percent annually between 1981 and 1985, the result of shifting cultivation, logging, and conversion to farms.

In countries where development opportunities for the majority have lagged, such as Ghana and the Philippines during the 1960s and 1970s, impoverished, often landless, rural households have moved into forested regions in search of arable land. In Ghana, a nation of 11 million people, over nine million hectares had come under shifting cultivation by 1980, 40 percent of the total land area and eight times the area of remaining productive forest.

Rules of land tenure in many countries that confer title to forest lands on parties who ''improve'' it by clearing the forest for some other use also invite deforestation. Brazilian authorities have tended to settle disputed Amazonian land claims by granting claimants title to areas that are multiples of the total forest area cleared for agricultural uses. In the Malaysian state of Sabah, laws dating from the British colonial period make the state government the holder of all forestry property rights, vitiating the traditional rights of local communities, but permit any native person to obtain title to forest land by clearing and cultivating it. In the Philippines, land claims predicated on forest clearance involve not only small-scale shifting cultivators, but also extensive livestock operations.

In Ghana, rights to use the resources of the forests were governed by traditional communities, until taken over by the central government in the early 1970s. As a result, the forest has become even more vulnerable, because tribal heads no longer have any strong incentive to limit shifting cultivation or timber operations. In many other countries as well, the displacement of traditional communities exercising customary law over the forest actually

weakened controls over resource use.

Much deforestation also stems directly from government policies in Third World countries toward forest exploitation, and toward industries that compete for the use of forest lands. Such policies overemphasize the timber harvest at the expense of other potential benefits and forego potential long-term benefits for lesser transitory gains. Potential benefits from forest exploitation are dissipated in wasteful harvesting and processing, or allowed to flow unnecessarily to stockholders of timber companies. Government policies also result in greater conversion of forest lands to agricultural and other uses than is economically warranted, with a loss in net benefits from the land. Despite official endorsements of conservation goals, government policies contribute significantly to the rapid deforestation now under way.

Why have these policies been adopted, and why do they persist? In many countries the policies were intended to reward special interest groups allied with or otherwise favored by those in power. The existence of large resource rents from harvesting mature timber has attracted politicians as well as businessmen to the opportunities for immediate gain.

That is not the whole story, however. To a considerable degree, the policy weaknesses identified in this study arose despite well-intentioned development objectives. The shortcomings have been failures of understanding and execution. The lessons of the succeeding chapters reveals six explanations for government policies that have erred in the direction of excessive forest depletion. In brief,

(1) Continuing benefits from intact natural forests have been consistently undervalued by both policymakers and the general public. An asset that is undervalued will inevitably be misused.

Forests have been exploited for a few valuable commodities, neglecting other tangible and intangible benefits. Natural forests serve protective as well as productive functions. Assigning money values to the protective services is much more difficult than estimating the market value of timber harvests. In addition, potential production has also been undervalued. Forests in the tropics have generally been exploited as if only two resources were of any significance: the timber and the agricultural land thought to lie beneath it. The capacity of the natural forest to supply a perpetual stream of valuable non-wood products that can be harvested without cutting down trees has been overlooked. In the tropics, these include such commodities as nuts, oils, fibers, plant and animal products with special uses. In advanced temperate zone countries, forests' recreational value is often underestimated.

(2) The net benefits from forest exploitation and conversion have been overestimated, both because the direct and indirect economic benefits have been exaggerated and because many of the costs have been ignored. Plans to harvest tropical logs every 35 years in cut-over stands have exaggerated the rate and extent of regeneration and have been grossly unfulfilled in Indonesia, the Philippines, and other countries studied. Assumptions about the agricultural potential from land underlying tropical forests have been even more optimistic, and results have been even more disappointing.

Policymakers have usually overestimated the employment and regional development benefits associated with timber industries, infrastructure investments, and agricultural settlements in tropical forests. Where such initiatives have not been economically sound to begin with, they

have not induced further development or even been able to sustain themselves without continuing dependence on government subsidies. However, one result of such inflated expectations has been that governments, both as holders of property rights in forests and as sovereign taxing authorities, have often allowed even the timber readily valued in world markets to be removed too cheaply— witness persistently low timber royalties and license fees and unduly low (sometimes zero) income and export taxes. Only in Sabah, (and then only after 1978) have governments been moderately successful in appropriating a sizable share of the rents available in logging. Elsewhere, sizable rents available to timber concessionaires have generated destructive timber booms and pressures for widespread, rapid exploitation.

An asset that is undervalued will inevitably be misused.

Nor have the employment benefits expected from forest utilization been realized. The wood products industries in tropical countries have provided some employment, to be sure, but with the single exception of Gabon, the timber sectors in tropical wood-exporting nations have typically provided jobs for less than 1 percent of the labor force, a figure only as high as in the diversified United States economy and half as high as in Canada. The attempt to expand employment, domestic value added, and foreign exchange earnings has led governments to protect domestic mills by banning log exports, imposing high export taxes on logs (but not on timber products), and granting tax and credit incentives. Jobs in the forest-based sector were indeed created, but at what cost to the nation? Large amounts of taxes and foreign exchange earnings were dissipated, and some of the sheltered industries became inefficient claimants to more of the forests than foreign mills could ever command. Similarly, the tendency

Sizable concessions to timber companies have generated destructive timber booms and pressures for widespread, rapid exploitation.

to underestimate not only the economic but also the social and environmental costs of forest exploitation has been pervasive. The destruction of habitat that threatens myriad little-known species endemic to tropical forests and the displacement or disturbance of indigenous communities have been especially neglected costs. In addition, the costs of the ''boom-town'' development that often arise from intensified logging and processing activities were overlooked in the drive to develop lagging or backward regions. In Indonesia, Brazil, and elsewhere, neither the infrastructure costs of providing for large inflows of immigrants to timber provinces in the early stages of timber booms nor the costs of maintaining excessive infrastructure in post-boom periods were viewed as offsets to the private economic benefits flowing from the opening of the natural forest. Instead, they were viewed as investments in regional development that could be financed through timber sales.

In some areas, large-scale extractive activity in natural forests has imposed heavy environmental costs. Misused, fragile tropical soils have been seriously damaged over large areas, for example. In Indonesia and the adjacent East Malaysian state of Sabah, these hitherto unforeseen costs reached calamitous heights in the drought year, 1983, when fires in both countries burned an area of closed tropical forest about one and one half times that of Taiwan. Previous droughts had brought fire, but on a far smaller scale. Extensive logging in both areas had by 1983 predisposed even the wet rain forest to disastrous fire damage, while unlogged forests suffered far milder damages. In Indonesia alone, losses from that fire in the value of the standing stock of trees exceeded US$5 billion, and the costs of ecological damage are still unknown.

(3) Development planners have proceeded too boldly to exploit tropical forests for commodity production without adequate biological knowledge of their potential or limitations or awareness of the economic consequences of development policies. Little is known about the potential commercial value of all but a very few of the tropical tree species, so most trees are treated as weeds and destroyed during logging. Much remains to be learned about potential regeneration of currently valuable tree species and successful management of heterogeneous tropical forests for sustained yields. Without this knowledge, loggers have blundered through the forests, extracting the few highly valued logs and severely damaging the rest. Even less is known of the potential value for agricultural, scientific, or medical purposes of the millions of other plant and animal species, despite clear indications from previous discoveries that forests may hold unknown treasures. Consequently, forest habitat is recklessly cleared to produce commodities of marginal economic value.

Large-scale agricultural settlements and livestock operations have been encouraged without adequate study of land use capabilities. Painful and costly failures have driven home the lesson that the lush tropical forest does not imply the existence of rich soils beneath it. It is now recognized that most underlying soils are too nutrient-poor for sustained crop production without heavy fertilization and that the better soils—along rivers, for example—are probably already being used by shifting cultivators. Similarly, massive conversions to monocultures and ranches have taken place without prior attention to potential problems of plant and animal diseases, pest and weed management, with costly and sometimes disastrous consequences. Only now is serious attention being paid to the capabilities of tropical soils and to the development of the sustainable farming and livestock systems suited to them.

Governments have pushed ahead with forest exploitation not only in advance of ecological knowledge but even before understanding the likely consequence of the policy instruments with which they hoped to stimulate development. Several countries awarded concessions for most of their productive forest estates before enough time had elapsed to assess properly the adequacy of their forest management system or the impact of forest revenue systems on licensees' behavior. Governments have stimulated large domestic processing industries before evaluating the appropriateness of the levels of protection afforded them, their technical and economic efficiency, and the costs and benefits to the national economy of the incentives provided. Similarly, governments have gone ahead with large-scale conversions of tropical forests before adequately evaluating the economic viability and the worth of the alternative uses.

(4) Policymakers have attempted without much success to draw on tropical forest resources to solve fiscal, economic, social and political conflicts elsewhere in society. In many countries, migration to forested regions has been seen as a means of relieving overcrowding and landlessness in settled agricultural regions, whether those conditions sprang from rapid population growth, highly concentrated land tenures, or slow growth of employment and opportunities for income generation. Rather than modifying development strategies to deal with employment creation and rural poverty, or tackling the politically difficult problem of land reform, many countries have used forests as an escape valve for demographic and economic pressures.

Sale of tropical timber assets has been seen as a ready means of raising government revenues and foreign exchange. Governments have found that drawing down these resources has been easier in the short run than broadening the tax base and improving tax administration or reversing trade policies that effectively penalize nascent export industries, though ultimately the assets and easy options are

Policymakers have attempted without much success to draw on tropical forest resources to solve fiscal, economic, social and political conflicts elsewhere in society.

exhausted and the underlying problems remain.

(5) National governments (and development assistance agencies) have been reluctant to invest enough resources in stewardship and management of the public forest resource, despite its enormous value. Development spending on the forest sector has been a tiny fraction of that allocated to agriculture. While most sizable countries in the Third World have built up substantial agricultural research programs (including tree crop research in some countries), none have developed appreciable research capabilities or activities focussed on natural forest ecology and management.

Despite the enormous value of the resource, including billions and in some countries even trillions of dollars in timber alone, and the large sums of money represented in the annual log harvest, governments have not built up adequate technical and economic expertise or effective management and enforcement capabilities. As countries with large petroleum and other mineral resources have found, the cost of such expertise and managerial capability is small relative to the value of the resource, and this investment is returned quickly in increased earnings to the national economy and the government treasury. Yet, the record of policy analysis in the forest sector is sparse, and infusions of funds and technical assistance to train, staff, equip, and monitor forest administration agencies have been inadequate.

(6) Finally, while national governments have overestimated their own capabilities for forest

management, they have underestimated the value of traditional management practices and local governance over forest resources. Local communities dependent on forests for many commodities and services, not just timber, have been more sensitive to their protective functions and the wide variety of goods available from them in a sustainable harvest. Moreover, when provincial and national governments have overruled traditional-use rights to the forests, local communities and individual households have been unable, and less willing, to prevent destructive encroachment or over-exploitation. Conversely, some governments have found that restoring or awarding such rights to local groups has induced them to attend to the possibilities of sustainable long-term production from forest resources.

Forest Sector Policies

Timber Concessions

Many tropical countries became independent still endowed with substantial public forests of mature commercial timber. Most have promoted rapid forest depletion by conceding much of their economic value to concessionaires that contract with the government to harvest the timber on public lands. Typically, the first contractors were foreign firms, some with links to former colonial powers. British, French, American, and more recently, Japanese, Korean, and Taiwanese firms have actively sought and implemented concession agreements. Still more recently, logging firms from Malaysia and the Philippines have won sizable concession areas in neighboring tropical countries. Over time, domestic entrepreneurs have taken increasingly important positions in highly profitable timber extraction, either as local partners to foreign companies or as sole concession holders. In Sabah, for example, a domestic foundation will ultimately become the sole concession holder, with foreign and domestic firms limited to the role of logging contractors.

The "stumpage value"[1] of an accessible virgin forest of commercial species is considerable.

This stumpage value is an economic rent, a value attributable not to any cost of production, but to the strength of market demand and favorable natural resource endowments and location. (See Table I.6.) For high-valued species, they were approximately US$70 to US$100 per cubic meter of logs at the end of the 1970s; for low-valued and middle-valued species, about one-quarter to one-half as much.

Rent, by definition, is a value in excess of the total costs of bringing trees to market as logs or wood products, including the cost of attracting the necessary investment. That cost may include a risk premium that reflects uncertainties about future market and political conditions, so there are inevitably doubts about the exact magnitude of available rent. Theoretically, all rent can be captured by governments as a revenue source that stems from the country's advantageous natural resource assets. In practice, royalties, land rents, license fees, and various harvest taxes are all means of converting rent into government revenues. To the extent it is not captured, a rent remains as a source of greater-than-normal profits for the timber contractor, or as a cushion for defraying excess costs.

In most developing countries with large mature forests, forest revenue systems don't come close to capturing these rents for the public treasury. While most countries have sought to raise the government's share over time, only some have been successful; in others, the real value of the government's revenues have been eroded by inflation, evasion, or poorly designed fiscal systems. Despite a variety of fees, royalties, taxes, and miscellaneous charges, total forest revenues have fallen far short of their potential in most exporting countries. (See Table I.7.) In the Philippines, the government captured only 16.5 percent of logging rents between 1979 and 1982, while Indonesia obtained 38 percent, as did Ghana in an earlier period. Of these countries, only Sabah's revenue system brought in a high percentage of potential revenues through aggressive taxation.

Table I.6. Estimated Rents in Logging Tropical Forests by Country, Species and Time Period

| Country and Period | Rents in Log Harvesting (US$ per m³) Value of Species | | | |
	Highest	Middle	Lowest	Overall
I. 1979				
Indonesia				85
Sabah, Malaysia				94
Philippines				69
Liberia	98	41		
II. 1973–74				
Indonesia				45
Liberia	89	58	25	
Ivory Coast	47	31	17	
Gabon	89	54	22	
Cameroon				
a) Douala	61	32	14	
b) Pointe Noire	52	23	7	
Congo				
a) South	81	52	23	
b) North	69	42	13	
III. 1971–72				
Ghana	79	28		

Source: Country case studies

The result of this failure has almost invariably been a rush by private contractors for (aptly named) "timber concessions," because those contracts for timber harvests and leases of public forest lands offer high potential rates of return on investment. The greater the loss of potential public revenues, the greater the profit incentive to private investors. Entrepreneurs are induced to seek timber concessions before others sign agreements to exploit all the profitable areas.

This rent-seeking behavior has generated the "timber booms" experienced by many countries. Foreign and domestic entrepreneurs contract for harvesting rights on vast areas. Sometimes to forestall risks of contract renegotiation or revision, and sometimes because of

This rent-seeking behavior has generated the "timber booms" experienced by many countries.

contractual obligations imposed by governments, concessionaires quickly enter the forests to begin large-scale harvesting operations. In part because royalties and other forest revenue systems encourage it, concessionaires typically "highgrade" their tracts, taking the best specimens of the most highly valued species but disturbing extensive forest areas in the process. Since access roads are vital to shifting cultivators and settlers, who rarely penetrate far into

Table I.7. Government Rent Capture in Tropical Timber Production $US millions

(1)	(2)	(3)	(4)	(5)	(6)
Country and Period	Potential Rent from Log Harvest	Actual Rent from Log Harvest	Official Government Rent Capture	(4) ÷ (3) (%)	(4) ÷ (2) (%)
Indonesia 1979–82	4,954	4,409	1,644	37.3	33.2
Sabah 1979–82	2,198	2,094	1,703	81.3	77.5
Ghana 1971–74	—	—	29	38.0	—
Philippines 1979–82	1,505	1,033	171	16.5	11.4

(1) Potential rent assumes that all harvested logs are allocated to uses (direct export, sawmills, plymills) that yield the largest net economic rent.

(2) Actual rent totals rents arising from the actual disposal of harvested logs.

(3) Rent capture totals timber royalties, export taxes, and other official fees and charges.

Source: Country case studies

wilderness forests, loggers are often quickly followed by migrants who complete the process of deforestation.

The Ivory Coast provides an extreme example. Despite *ad valorem* export taxes that ranged from 25 percent of f.o.b. value for low-valued species to 45 percent for highly prized varieties, the estimated rents left to concessionaires during the 1970s approximated US$40 per cubic meter for the most valuable species, US$30 for moderate valued species, and US$20 for low-valued varieties. *(See Table I.6.)* These were more than sufficient to stimulate rapid exploitation and depletion of the timber resource. Between 1965 and 1972, concession agreements assigned more than two-thirds of all productive forests to concessionaires within seven years.

Concessionaires typically "highgrade" their tracts, taking the best specimens of the most highly valued species but disturbing extensive forest areas in the process.

Timber contractors have virtually exhausted the more valuable species, and shifting cultivators have moved in on their heels to clear the depleted forests. In 1985, Ivorian forests amounted to only 22 percent of their extent 30 years earlier. Ominously, the rents per cubic meter are much lower in the Ivory Coast than those available to concessionaires in countries such as Gabon, where considerable reserves still remain.

Detailed estimates for Indonesia illustrate the size and disposition of rents. Log exports from Sumatra and Kalimantan, two main concession areas, generated potential rents that averaged US$62 per cubic meter exported between 1979 and 1982. This figure is the logs' average export value minus the total costs of harvesting and transporting them (exclusive of taxes and fees). Total identifiable government revenues, including timber royalties, land taxes, reforestation fees and other charges, averaged US$28 per cubic meter. Thus, the government recaptured only 45 percent of the rents available from log exports.

Timber exported as sawn timber received even more favorable treatment. Due to lower tax rates intended to encourage local processing, the government captured only 21 percent of the rents generated by Indonesian logs exported as sawn timber. Potential rents from logs used for plywood production were actually destroyed because production costs exceeded the price margin between log and plywood exports, so that, without tax concessions and investment incentives, plywood producers would have incurred losses. Between 1979 and 1982 the potential economic rents generated by log production, whether for further processing or direct export, exceeded US$4.95 billion. Of this, the government's share, collected through official taxes and fees, was US$1.65 billion. Five hundred million dollars of potential profits were lost because relatively high-cost domestic processing generated negative economic returns. The remainder, US$2.8 billion, was left to private parties. This represents an average of US$700 million in rents annually. Not all of this accrued to concessionaires. According to widespread reports, politicians, military officers, forestry officials, and local civil authorities have shared in the windfall. Largely because of such strong profit incentives, by 1985 the total area under more

than 500 concession agreements or being awarded to applicants was 65.4 million hectares, 1.4 million hectares more than the total area of production forests in the country.

In the Philippines, between 1979 and 1982, the forest sector generated rents in excess of a billion dollars. The potential rents were even larger, approximately US$1.5 billion. The difference is the loss due to conversion of an increasing volume of exportable logs to plywood in inefficient mills. As discussed in more detail below, the low conversion rates in Filipino mills implied that each log exported as plywood brought a lower net return over cost than the same log exported as sawn timber or without processing. By comparison, the government's total revenues over these years from export taxes and forest charges on log, timber, and plywood production was US$171 million, less than 12 percent of potential rents and 17 percent of actual available rents. The remainder, more than 820 million dollars, was retained by exploiters of the forest resource.

Moreover, although the production cost estimates needed to estimate aggregate rents for earlier periods aren't available, it appears that before 1979, when timber harvests in the Philippines were at a higher level, the government's share of rents generated by forest exploitation was even lower. From 1979 to 1982, forest charges and export taxes totaled 11 percent of the value of forest product exports. In the preceding five years, they came to only 8 percent.

The result in the Philippines was also a dramatic timber boom. Between 1960 and 1970, the area under concession agreements rose rapidly from about 4.5 to 10.5 million hectares. Many large U.S. timber companies participated, along with increasing involvement by the Philippines' military, political, and traditional elites. Logging activity rose in step, peaking in the mid-1970s. By the mid-1980s, virgin productive forests had virtually been logged out.

Many governments have reinforced these powerful incentives for timber exploitation with other provisions that accelerate the process. Governments enter agreements with concessionaires, not through competitive bidding, which would increase the government's share of the rents, but on the basis of standard terms or individually negotiated agreements. Potential investors thus rush into agreements before others take up all the favorable sites offered for exploitation.

Governments typically require concessionaires to begin harvesting their sites within a stipulated time, and also limit agreements to periods much shorter than a single forest rotation: to 25, 20, 10, 5, and even a single year. In Sabah, for example, half of all timber leases are for the regular 21-year term, but most of the remainder are for only 10 years, and 5 percent are for just one year. These conditions are imposed to prevent concessionaires from stockpiling leases, but result in a much faster harvest schedule and less concern for future productivity than the private investor would choose if he owned the land and the timber outright and had to pay only an ordinary income tax. In Indonesia, though logging regulations prescribe that 35 years should elapse after the initial harvest before tracts are reentered for a second cut, to allow sufficient regeneration and growth, standard concession agreements are for only 20 years. Concessionaires in Indonesia have often reentered forests for a second cut long before the stand has had an adequate chance to recover, in order to strip the forest of remaining merchantable timber before the concession expires.

Macroeconomic policies, such as exchange rate overvaluation and undervaluation, may affect timber rents. In Indonesia, for example, the rupiah was allowed to appreciate against the U.S. dollar by more than 50 percent between 1970 and 1977, before a currency devaluation in 1978 partially restored the earlier relationship. The cycle was repeated between 1979 and 1983. These episodes of currency overvaluation reduced private rents from tim-

ber exports. But, they may have more severely discouraged non-timber forest product exports, because their supply costs are determined mostly by domestic labor costs.

In Ghana, between 1977 and 1980, the free market exchange rate varied between 5 and 8 times the official exchange rate. Such extreme currency overvaluation discouraged all export production, except that which could be smuggled out. For those years, timber smuggled overland is estimated to have earned 80 percent as much foreign exchange as timber exported officially, but without contributing to tax receipts. Inadvertently, government revenues and management control over the public forests were reduced along with export earnings.

Of course, countries sometimes maintain undervalued exchange rates, which have the opposite effect. Exports of forest products are encouraged by payments to shippers in domestic currency in excess of the value of the foreign exchange they earn. Malaysia's currency has consistently been undervalued, stimulating logging and conversion of vast logged-over areas to plantations of such export tree crops as rubber and palm oil.

In addition, some governments increase the potential rents available to contractors on timber from public lands by assuming some of the costs of bringing timber to market. These include costs of constructing trunk roads, port facilities, and other infrastructure; administrative costs of surveying, marking, and grading timber to be sold; and costs due to the environmental side effects of timber operations.

In extreme cases, budgetary subsidies permit the commercial harvest of timber that has negative rent; i.e., timber that is not worth marketing. In the United States, for example, the Forest Service supports logging on over 100 million acres of the national forests that are economically unfit for sustained timber production. It does so by selling timber at prices below its own growing, road building, harvest-

> *In extreme cases, budgetary subsidies permit the commercial harvest of timber that is not worth marketing. In the United States, for example, the Forest Service supports logging on over 100 million acres of the national forests that are economically unfit for sustained timber production—at a cost to taxpayers of about 100 million dollars a year.*

ing, and selling expenses, at a cost to taxpayers of about 100 million dollars a year. Although the Forest Service tries to justify this policy in terms of its benefits to wildlife and recreation, these subsidies reflect an undue precedence for timber production over other management objectives in most U.S. national forests.

Governments affect the pace of deforestation both by the level of their logging charges in public forests, and by the form those charges take. The structure of forest revenue systems can markedly affect the pattern and level of harvesting, as well as the division of rents between government and concessionaire. (Gray 1983.) Most forest charges are based on the volume of timber removed, not the volume of merchantable timber in the tract. Along with high transport costs and narrow market preferences for known species, this approach encourages licensees to harvest highly selectively, taking only the most valuable stems. Consequently, a larger area must be harvested to meet timber demands, opening up more of the forest to shifting cultivators and the remaining trees are usually severely damaged by logging operations. In Sabah, between 45 and 74 percent of trees remaining after logging are substantially damaged or destroyed; in Indonesia and the Philippines, estimates of damage fall in the same range. If concessionaires reenter tracts within 5 to 10 years to

extract any remaining valuable timber before their licenses expire, they leave the forest virtually valueless and so badly damaged that regeneration is uncertain. In the Ivory Coast, between 1962 and 1978 highly valued species (including ebony and mahogany) almost disappeared from the forests while the percentage of "other" low-valued trees in timber exports rose dramatically from 15 to over 50 percent of the harvest. (Arnaud, 1980)

Inappropriately designed forest revenue systems encourage high-grading of timber stands. Of the many forms timber charges take, flat charges per cubic meter harvested provide licensees the strongest incentive for high-grading, unless they are finely differentiated by species, grade, and site condition. *Ad valorem* royalties are better than flat charges but not by much. The reason is simple: trees with a stumpage value less than the forest charge are worthless to the licensee, and can be left or destroyed with impunity. The Philippines government charges licensees a relatively undifferentiated specific royalty that tends to encourage high-grading. Finely differentiated systems are not widely used because they are beyond the administrative capabilities of most tropical countries. However, the Malaysian state of Sarawak imposes specific charges that vary considerably by species, with much lower rates on low-valued trees, and suffers only half as much residual tree damage from logging operations as Sabah and Indonesia. If such differentiated systems are administratively infeasible, revenue systems based on ground rents (area license fees) promote more complete utilization of the growing timber because even inferior trees are more likely to have some positive stumpage value.[2]

As important as the terms of forestry concession agreements is their enforcement, which is inherently difficult. Forested regions are vast and remote. What happens there is far removed from public scrutiny. Even in countries such as Liberia that have used forest guards, government agents are thinly spread and forest exploitation provides ample funds for bribes. In many countries, including the Philippines, Malaysia, and Indonesia, timber concessionaires have been closely linked to political or military leaders, which makes enforcement by mere forest agents difficult. When concession terms are not adequately enforced, concessionaires can cut costs and raise their returns, usually at the expense of the government and the forest resource base. In the Ivory Coast, for example, harvest methods were not even prescribed in concession agreements until 1972. Thereafter, through the 1970s, forestry officials lacked the resources and the information required to determine and enforce annual allowable cuts, obligatory removal of secondary species, or to verify the working programs of logging companies. As a result, concessionaires were not obliged to follow any particular technique of selection, nor any particular cutting methods.

In the Philippines, illegal cutting and timber smuggling have been widespread. During the 1970s, restrictions on log exports were introduced to encourage local processing and to preserve timber resources. From 1976 on, for example, log exports were allowed only from certain regions and in 1979 were limited to 25 percent of the total annual allowable cut. The result was considerable log smuggling and underreporting of exports. Between 1977 to 1979, Japanese trade data recorded imports of 4.7 million cubic meters from the Philippines, but the Philippines' recorded exports to Japan, where three fourths of forest products exports were sent, totaled only 4.1 million cubic meters, a discrepancy worth US$70 million in export receipts. In 1980, after log export restrictions were tightened, the incentive to smuggle out logs became stronger. A glut of logs on the domestic market kept prices within the Philippines much below prices on the export market. Correspondingly, the discrepancy in reported exports widened: Japan imported 1.1 million cubic meters of logs from the Philippines, although only 0.5 million were recorded as Filipino exports. Indonesia has experienced similar problems of log smuggling, underreporting of harvests, and evasion of forestry

stipulations and export bans. In 1985 the official reported timber harvest was about 15 million cubic feet, but data aggregated from processors and shippers suggested a total of over 25 million cubic feet.

Incentives for Wood-Processing Industries

Log-exporting countries have had to struggle to establish local wood-processing industries, even though processing reduces the weight of the raw material and economizes on shipping costs. One important reason is that most industrial countries have set tariffs much higher on imports of processed wood products than on logs so as to protect their own wood manufacturing industries. *(See Table I.8.)* Such tariff escalation allows protected industries to compete successfully even if their labor and capital costs are much higher. Indeed, studies of wood-processing industries in Japan and Europe show that without trade protection their costs would be uncompetitive. (Contreras 1982.) Removal of these trade barriers would increase world trade and welfare.

To counteract these tariff barriers and to stimulate investment in processing capacity that would create employment and value-added in wood industries, log-exporting countries have banned log exports, reduced or waived export taxes on processed wood, and offered substantial investment incentives to forest product industries. Ghana used four different measures in the attempt to stimulate investment in domestic processing industries: log export bans were enacted (but mostly evaded); plywood and other wood products were exempted from export taxes (which were far less onerous than the currency overvaluation); long-term loans for sawmills and plymills were granted at zero or negative real interest rates; and, finally, a 50-percent rebate on income tax liabilities was given to firms that exported more than 25 percent of output. By 1982, these policies had created a domestic industry comprising 95 sawmills, 10 veneer and plywood plants, and 30 wood-processing plants.

Table I.8. Most Favored Nation (MFN) Tariff Levels for Selected Forest Products: Australia, EEC, Japan, USA (as of December 1985)

CCCN Tariff No.	General Product Description	Tariff Rate (%)			
		Australia	EEC	Japan	USA
44.03	Wood in rough	0	0	0	0
44.05	Wood simply sawn	5	0,4.1	0,7,10	0
44.09	Wood chips	0	0	0	0
44.13	Wood planed, grooved etc.	0–15	0,4.1	10	0,4.4
44.14	Veneer	5	6.1	15	0
44.15	Plywood	30–40	10.4	15,20	4.1–20
	Laminated lumber	15	11.1	20 +3.4%	1.9c/lb.
44.19 to 44.28	Manufacture of wood products	15	2.6–9.1	2.5–7.2	0–8
44.01 to 44.03	Furniture	30	5.6,6.3	4.8	4.7–9.3
47.01	Wood pulp	0	0	0	0
48.01 to 48.15	Newsprint	7	5.4	3.9	0
	Other paper and paperboard	6–14	4.1–12.8	5–12	0–3.3

Notes: These are MFN rates. Special preferences may be available for specified supplying countries, products are eligible for GSP treatment. Non-tariff barriers may place limitations on some products.

Source: Bourke 1984

Similarly, in the Ivory Coast generous incentives were given for creation of wood processing capacity. Firms making approved investments can write off half the costs against income tax liabilities and are eligible for income tax holidays for seven to eleven years on subsequent profits. These incentives, in addition to the large reductions in export taxes on exports of processed wood, explain the creation of a sizable but inefficient processing industry.

During the 1970s, Brazil offered liberal subsidies to wood-processing industries in the Ama-

zon, within a framework of generous incentives to encourage Amazonian investments. Firms were offered tax credits equal to their investments in approved projects, up to 50 percent of their total income tax liability and 75 percent of total project costs. In other words, firms could use money owed in taxes to invest in the Amazon. Between 1965 and 1983, about a half billion dollars of such funds were invested in wood-processing industries—35 percent of all tax credit funds committed to Amazonian investments. In addition, approved projects enjoyed partial or complete income tax holidays for up to 15 years. By 1983, the agency administering these incentive programs had granted tax holidays to 260 wood processing firms in the Amazon. Finally, Amazonian wood producers and traders have received liberal export financing. From 1981 to 1985, export trading companies were eligible for subsidized credits up to 100 percent of their exports in the prior year at interest rates well below the rate of inflation, a subsidy of up to 30 percent on forest product exports.

Such industrial incentives can increase local employment, but often do so at a heavy cost in lost government revenues and faster deforestation. In Ghana, Ivory Coast, and Indonesia, many of the mills established in response to these inducements have been small and inefficient. Conversion rates of logs into sawn lumber and plywood have been only about two thirds of industry standards. Shifting to domestic processing in technically inefficient mills means that considerably more logs must be harvested to meet any level of demand, disturbing much larger forest areas through selective cutting.

Furthermore, after governments have encouraged investments in local processing industries, officials are most reluctant to reduce their raw material supply. This stance virtually ensures that enough logs will continue to be harvested to feed the mills, whatever the economic or ecological reasons for reducing the harvest. In the United States, one of the main reasons why the U.S. Forest Service continues to harvest timber on lands unsuitable for commercial production is to supply local mills dependent on logs from the national forests.

The Indonesian case illustrates the fiscal costs and risks to the forests that ambitious forest-based industrialization entails. To encourage local processing, the government raised the log export tax rate to 20 percent in 1978, exempting most sawn timber and all plywood. Mills were also exempted from income taxes for five or six years. Since these tax holidays were combined with unlimited loss-carryover provisions, con-

cessionaires were frequently able to extend the holiday by declaring (unaudited) losses during the five-year holiday provision, or by simply arguing before sympathetic tax officials that the holidays were intended to apply for five years after the start of profitable operations.

With these incentives and the impending ban on log exports, the number of operating or planned sawmills and plymills jumped from 16 in 1977 to 182 in 1983. By 1988, plymills will be on stream with a total installed capacity for processing 20 million cubic meters of logs per year. Sawmill capacity is expected to account for another 18 million cubic meters of logs, of which only 1 million cubic meters will be met from teak plantations on Java. As much as 37 million could come from the natural forests, an annual harvest level 50 percent greater than the maximum levels reached in the 1970s, when log exports peaked. But, according to Government of Indonesia long-term forestry plans, log harvests to feed the mills are expected to continue rising throughout the 1990s as well.

Because of low conversion efficiencies and distortions in relative log and plywood prices in world markets, the jobs this harvest will create are bought at a heavy cost. For example, although a cubic meter of plywood could be exported for US$250 in 1983, the export value in terms of the logs used as raw materials (the roundwood equivalent) was only US$109. However, the logs themselves could be exported for US$100 per cubic meter. In other words, plymills added only US$9 in export earnings for every cubic meter of logs used. But, because of the export tax exemption for plywood, the government sacrificed US$20 in foregone tax revenues on every cubic meter of logs diverted to plymills. At current prices and conversion rates and projected production levels, by 1988 the revenue loss would mount to US$400 million annually. In 1983, plywood exports worth US$109 at international prices per cubic meter of logs processed cost the rupiah equivalent of US$133 to produce, a sacrifice of potential gains possible only because of the government's financial incentives and its forgiveness of log export taxes.

The losses involved in producing sawn timber for export were more obvious. Because the average price of sawn timber exported in 1983 was only US$155, a cubic meter of logs that could be exported for US$100 brought only US$89 if processed in local sawmills. The government actually sacrificed US$20 in export taxes in order to lose US$11 in export earnings on every cubic meter of logs sawn domestically. Economic losses, as well as the waste of the natural resources and the sacrifice of public revenues, can result when overly generous incentives permit or encourage inefficient processing operations.

Although the data are less complete than in Indonesia, other countries' industrial policies raise the same issues. In the Philippines, a large processing sector was created by fiscal incentives, by threatening bans on log exports, by linking logging concessions to industrial investments, and by differential export taxes. By 1980, some 209 plymills were operating, with an annual log input of 3.4 million cubic meters. Most were small and inefficient, with an average conversion rate of only 43 percent, compared to 55 percent in Japan, though lower labor and transport costs partly offset this disadvantage.

From 1981 through 1983, production costs in Filipino plymills exceeded export receipts on logs converted to plywood so that rents were actually dissipated. Nonetheless, private interests could profit because of investment incentives and log export tax relief, which alone amounted to US$18 per cubic meter of logs sent to domestic plymills. Although the number of mills dropped over these years through consolidation and rationalization in the plywood industry, enough capacity remained in 1982 to process 3.1 million cubic meters of logs.

In the Ivory Coast, plymills have been erected by timber concessionaires mainly to qualify for log export quotas and are widely regarded as inefficient, with conversion ratios of about 40 percent. Because *ad valorem* export taxes on plywood are only 1 to 2 percent, instead of 25 to 45 percent for the logs themselves, domestic processing involves a considerable sacrifice of government revenues. *(See Table I.9.)* For *iroko*, for example, more than US$50 in taxes are foregone for every US$25 of extra foreign exchange earnings generated when a cubic meter of log is processed into plywood.

In summary, excessive incentives to forest product industries that encourage rapid, often inefficient, investment in wood-processing capacity, combine with inappropriate concession agreements to increase the log harvest much beyond what it would otherwise be. Poorly drafted and enforced forestry stipulations can't ensure sustainable forestry practices in the face of these powerful incentives. Forest stocks are depleted, but neither the government treasury nor the national economy benefit much from the exploitation.

Indeed, many unmeasured costs reduce the benefits even further. In all the countries studied, settlers and shifting cultivators travel the logging roads after the log harvest, clearing the remaining forest after the commercial stems have been removed. Deforestation by shifting cultivators and timber operations are closely interlinked.

With forest clearance, the production of many forest products other than timber is reduced, which have an important, usually underestimated, aggregate value. The exports alone of such products from Indonesia— including rattan, resin, honey, natural silk, sandalwood, nuts and fruits, cosmetic and pharmaceutical products—reached US$120 million in 1982. There was substantial domestic consumption as well. The value of these exports was nearly half as large as the Indonesian government's total revenues from timber exports. In addition, ecological losses are severe. The most dramatic were suffered in

Table I.9. Ivory Coast: Export Taxes and Incentives

Species	Additional Domestic Value-Added From Sawmilling US Percent (per m³)	Export Taxes Foregone by Government on Sawn Timber Exports (per m³)	Taxes Foregone as % of Increased Value-Added
Iroko	25.50	52.00	204
Acajou	19.20	43.00	224
Llomba	9.24	10.00	108

Source: Country case study

Indonesia and Sabah during the 1982 to 1993 drought. Intense forest fires destroyed an area in East Kalimantan as large as all of Belgium—the worst forest fire ever recorded. Less is known about the extent of losses in Sabah, but damage was very extensive. Destruction in both countries was especially severe in logged over areas, because dead trees and litter provided enough fuel to ignite remaining stems. Damage to unlogged areas was slight. Such ecological disasters, along with soil erosion and compaction, river siltation and flooding, and destruction of the habitats of indigenous peoples and wild species, are among the unpriced costs of these incentives for forest exploitation.

Policies Outside the Forest Sector

In many countries non-forestry policies have caused greater forest destruction than misdirected and misapplied forestry policies have. Non-forestry policies prejudicial to forest conservation may be arranged on a continuum that ranges from self-evident to subtle. Most obvious are the effects of policies leading directly to physical intrusion in natural forest areas. These include agricultural programs under which forest land is cleared for such estate crops as rubber, palm oil, cacao, for annual crops, and even for fish ponds. Closely related are public investments in mining,

dams, roads, and other large infrastructure projects that incidentally result in significant, once-and-for-all destruction of forest resources. Many such projects are politically driven and of questionable economic worth, even apart from the forest and other natural resource losses they impose.

Further along the continuum are tax, credit, and pricing policies that stimulate private investments in competing land uses. Many governments have deliberately adopted policies that accelerate the conversion of forest lands to farming or ranching, through incentives that artificially lower the costs and increase the private profitability of the alternative land uses. These subsidies can become so large that they encourage activities that are intrinsically uneconomic or push alternative land uses beyond the limits of economic rationality. When this happens, inferior and often unsustainable land uses are established, only because of the subsidies.

Next on the continuum are land-tenure policies that encourage deforestation. Of these, the most direct are tenurial rules that assign property rights over public forests to private parties on condition that such lands are "developed" or "improved." Such rules have facilitated small farmer expansion into forested regions, but in some countries have been used by wealthier parties to amass large holdings. A

In many countries non-forestry policies have caused greater forest destruction than misdirected and misapplied forestry policies have.

few countries, including China, have demonstrated that this policy works in reverse, by awarding private tenures to deforested public wastelands on condition that they be reforested.

A more indirect tenurial policy has been the centralization of proprietary rights to forest lands in national governments, superceding traditional rights of local authorities and communities. Although intended to strengthen control, such actions have more often undermined local rules governing access and use, removed local incentives for conservation, and saddled central governments with far-flung responsibilities beyond their administrative capabilities.

Finally, the furthest points on the continuum represent those policies that appear at first glance to have few implications for forest use, but which ultimately prove to be significant sources of policy-induced forest destruction. Included here are all domestic policies that further impoverish households living close to the margin of subsistence, especially in rural areas. These include pricing policies and investment priorities biased against agriculture, development strategies that depress the demand for unskilled labor, and farm policies that favor large farmers over smallholders. These policies retard the demographic transition, make rural populations more dependent on natural forests for subsistence needs, and increase the concentration of agricultural landholdings.

Subsidy programs take several forms. Governments may assume many of the costs of establishing the competing activity through spending on infrastructure, grants to settlers, or losses in state-operated enterprises. Governments provide financial aid to private investors through low-interest loans and tax breaks. Also, governments boost the profitability of agriculture or ranching by manipulating farm prices. All such measures shift the margin of relative profitability between forestry and the competing land use, and encourage more forest conversion than would otherwise take place.

In many forest-rich countries, governments actively promote and subsidize agricultural settlements in forested areas, often at very heavy cost. Multilateral development banks and bilateral aid agencies have shared these costs. In Indonesia, for example, the "transmigration" of settlers from Java to the heavily forested, sparsely populated Outer Islands is a long-standing government program. In the 1970s, approximately one million people were moved, at a cost of several thousand dollars per family. Between 1983 and 1988, the government of Indonesia plans to resettle 1 million families, about 5 million additional people, and government's costs have risen to US$10,000 per household. This is an extraordinarily high subsidy in a country where 1985 GNP per capita was only US$530 per year and total annual investment per capita is only US$125. The World Bank has loaned hundreds of millions of dollars to Indonesia to support the transmigration program.

In the past, many of these settlements have failed, in part because of inadequate assessment of the agricultural capabilities of the soils in the Outer Islands. Despite their low population densities, they do not offer large areas of good, unutilized agricultural land. For the most part, their tropical soils are nutrient-poor, easily leached, and erodible. Most of the nutrients are held in the biomass or the first inch or two of soil, so the process of clearing the forest often impoverishes the land. Low population densities broadly reflect the Outer Islands' limited agricultural potential, just as Java's dense population is due to its deep, fertile, volcanic soils. For the most part, the better agricultural lands in the Outer Islands are already occupied, and land conflicts between Javanese transmigrants and the linguistically and culturally distinct indigenous populations have been chronic. (Repetto 1986.)

Partly for this reason, 80 percent of new transmigrants are to be settled in logged and unlogged forests. Their holdings are to consist largely of rubber, oil palm, and other commercial tree crops, supplementing subsistence crop production. This agronomic system may avoid some of the crop failures, soil depletion, and marketing gaps that accompanied efforts to introduce Javanese rice-dominated cropping patterns to ecologically different areas. But, if targets are met, it will still mean the conversion of about 3 million hectares of forest land by 1988, an area equal to 5 percent of all productive forests.

Converting tropical forests to plantation crops can indeed raise income and employment. Since 1950, peninsular Malaysia has converted 12 percent of its forest area to establish over a million hectares of permanent crops, such as rubber and oil palm, and become a leading exporter of these commodities. With fertilizers, plantation crop yields are sustainable and provide continuous soil cover. Whether or not Indonesia's revised transmigration program will be as successful is uncertain, but it clearly promotes a rate of conversion greater than that which spontaneous migration and investment would bring about in the absence of large government subsidies.

The government of Brazil has engaged in even more massive efforts to colonize its tropical forests with small farmers, despite generally unsuccessful past experiences—along the Transamazon Highway, for example. The Northwest Development Programme (Polonoroeste) encompasses the entire State of Rondônia and part of Mato Grosso, an area where spontaneous settlement has been occurring for decades. The government undertook to demarcate plots and establish land titles. By mid-1985 the responsible agency had awarded 30,000 titles,

most for 100 hectare farms, but tens of thousands of other households are awaiting titles on homesteads they have established. Settlers pay only nominal title fees for their land, can recover their relocation costs by selling timber, and become eligible for subsidized agricultural credits. Heavy government outlays in road building, agricultural development, and other infrastructure have accelerated immigration. The budget for Polonoroeste for 1981 to 1986 exceeded one billion dollars, and the World Bank has concluded loans for more than US$400 million to support the program. Total spending has reached an estimated US$12,000 per settler family. (Aufderheide and Rich 1985).

World Bank lending has been conditional on the creation of Indian reserves, a national park, ecological stations, and biological reserves, and restriction of agricultural settlements to suitable agricultural soils, which have been estimated to underlie a third of the region. However, these conditions have not been met. Incursions on Indian territories, rapid deforestation, and uncontrolled immigration have taken place. In 1984, some 140,000 new settlers were arriving in Rondonia per year. Many have found that their cleared plots cannot support perennial agriculture and have abandoned them or sold them to cattle ranchers. As in Indonesia, these conversions of forested areas would not take place at nearly their present rate without heavy public expenditure.

Besides directly sponsoring agricultural settlements, many governments have provided generous indirect subsidies to activities that encroach on the forests. In Latin America, incentives for cattle ranching are the main example: they have resulted in the deforestation of enormous areas. Many of the ranches that were established have been uneconomic, and probably would not have been established without heavy subsidies and the hope of speculative gains in land prices. Sparse, deteriorating pastures far from markets have not supported enough cattle to justify the costs of planting and maintaining them. Many of these deforested lands have been sold or abandoned,

> *In Latin America, incentives for cattle ranching have resulted in the deforestation of enormous areas. Many of the ranches established have been uneconomic, and probably would not have been established without heavy subsidies and the hope of speculative gains in land prices.*

while new lands are cleared for the tax benefits they offer.

In Brazil, the Amazon's cattle herd had reached almost 9 million head by 1980. At an average stocking rate of one head per hectare, conversion to pasturage for cattle ranching had accounted for 72 percent of all the forest alteration detected by Landsat monitoring up to that time. Almost 30 percent of this conversion is attributable to several hundred large-scale, heavily subsidized ranches. By 1983, some 470 cattle projects averaging 23,000 hectares each had been approved by the Superintendencia do Desenvolvimento da Amazon (SUDAM) and had received financial assistance. On average, they had converted 5,500 hectares to pasture. As mentioned in the discussion of the Brazilian wood-processing industry, tax credits could contribute up to 75 percent of the capital requirements of a project if the parent company had other tax liabilities to offset. These capital grants have totaled more than US$500 million in tax forgiveness, more than 40 percent of the total amount conferred on all Amazon investments. They have been reinforced with credits at negative interest rates that represented an 85 to 95 percent discount from commercial interest rates over the 1970s.[3] Generous income-tax holidays and depreciation allowances, combined with low overall tax rates on agricultural incomes, effectively exempted such projects from income-tax liabilities, while operating losses could be written off against income from other sources.

Furthermore, after 1980, when rising credit and transport costs squeezed smaller operations, the SUDAM-assisted projects took on even more importance. According to survey data comparing these ranches with a sample of unassisted operations, four times as much of the deforestation attributable to subsidized ranches has occurred after 1980 as that attributable to unassisted projects. The subsidized ranches have large areas of forest still uncleared and are establishing more new pastures than unassisted ranchers. One reason is that the subsidies discourage continuing outlays to combat weeds and maintain soil fertility, outlays that are usually not eligible for capital grants, and encourage capital expenditures for establishing new pastures, which are eligible. A survey of SUDAM-assisted ranches estimated that 22 percent of the cleared area had already been abandoned or left to fallow by 1985.

The overall economic worth of these large SUDAM-assisted ranching projects is highly questionable, though more than 50,000 unsubsidized ranches in the Amazon in 1980 show that ranching is economically viable in some areas and circumstances. Since initial capital costs for land clearing, pasture development, and stocking are approximately US$400 per hectare, and gross revenues are only about US$60 per hectare once the ranch is operating, returns must be marginal, at best.

An economic and financial evaluation of a typical 20,000-hectare cattle ranch of the 1970s, based on sample survey data and reported more fully in the Brazilian case study, contrasted its intrinsic economic returns with its profitability to a private investor able to take advantage of the incentives and subsidies available to projects in the Amazon during the 1970s (and continuing in large part to the present). Even under optimistic assumptions, the typical cattle project is an extremely poor investment. *(See Table 1.10.)* In the base case, which assumes a 15-year project life, after which land, cattle, and equipment are sold, an annual rise in land values 2 percent above the

Table I.10. Economic and Financial Analysis of Government-Assisted Cattle Ranches in the Brazilian Amazon

	Net Present Value (US$)	Total Investment Outlay (US$)	NPV: Investment Outlay
I. Economic Analysis			
A. Base case	−2,824,000	5,143,700	−.55
B. Sensitivity Analysis			
1. Cattle prices assumed doubled	511,380	5,143,700	+.10
2. Land prices assumed rising 5%/year more than general inflation rate	−2,300,370	5,143,700	−.45
II. Financial Analysis			
A. Reflecting all investor incentives: tax credits, deductions, and subsidized loans	1,875,400	753,650	+2.49
B. Sensitivity Analysis			
1. Interest rate subsidy eliminated	849,000	753,650	+1.13
2. Deductibility of losses from other taxable income also eliminated	−658,500	753,650	−0.87

Source: Brazil country case study.

general rate of inflation, and a real discount rate of about 5 percent, the present value of the investment is a loss equal to 55 percent of total investment costs. Economic losses are US$2.8 million out of a total investment cost of US$5.1 million for the typical ranch. Sensitivity analysis shows that even if land prices rose annually at 5 percentage points above the inflation rate, the typical ranch would still lose 45 percent of invested capital. Even if cattle prices were doubled, the project would only be marginally viable. In other words, these ranches, which have converted millions of hectares of tropical forest, are intrinsically bad investments.

The second panel in Table I.10 explains why these investments nonetheless went ahead. It presents their returns, not to the national economy, but to the private entrepreneur able to take advantage of all the incentives. Even though intrinsically uneconomic, the project has a present value to the private investor equal to 249 percent of his equity input, at a real discount rate of 5 percent. Sensitivity analysis shows that this present value remains positive if interest rate subsidies are removed, but turns negative if provisions for offsetting operating losses against other taxable income are also withdrawn. The implication is that government policy made profitable investments that were intrinsically uneconomic and that led to the conversion of large areas of tropical forest to pasturage of low productivity for livestock operations.

The fiscal burden of Brazil's program has also been heavy. The government has had to

In Brazil, government policy made profitable investments that were intrinsically uneconomic and that led to the conversion of large areas of tropical forest to pasturage of low productivity for livestock operations.

provide, one way or another, both the resources to absorb losses and those to provide large profits to private investors. For the typical ranch, the present value of the government's total financial contribution is US$5.6 million (twice the cost the government would have incurred had it undertaken the investment directly). For all 470 SUDAM-assisted ranches, the estimated total fiscal cost is US$2.5 billion.

Other countries also provide fiscal incentives for investment in activities that compete with forests for land. In the Philippines, approved projects are eligible for (1) exemptions from duties on imported capital equipment and equivalent tax credits on equipment obtained domestically, (2) tax deductions for transportation, training, and research costs, (3) unlimited loss carry-forward against future taxable income, (4) accelerated depreciation, and (5) such additional benefits as eligibility for credit at concessional rates. In the Philippines, however, the few agricultural projects that have been approved for investment incentives have not drawn significantly on the area of productive forests. The scale of subsidized forest conversion for cattle ranching in the Brazilian Amazon is probably unique.

Conclusions and Recommendations

Many governments of countries endowed with rich forest resources have created economic incentives that stimulate rapid depletion of the timber resource and encourage the conversion of forest land to agricultural and other uses. Although such policies have been adopted in the name of development, the issue is not between economic development and resource conservation. Most are unsuccessful when judged only as means to promote economic growth. They result in huge economic losses: wastage of resources, excessive costs, reductions in potential profits and net foreign exchange earnings, loss of badly needed government revenues, and unearned windfalls for a few favored businesses and individuals.

They also result in severe environmental losses: unnecessary destruction and depletion of valuable forest resources; displacement of indigenous peoples, degradation of soils, waters, and ecosystems; and loss of habitat for many wildlife species. Both development and environmental goals can be served by policy improvements described in this report.

Policies that are the responsibility of the governments that own the forests or regulate activities in them, and those that are the responsibility of agencies representing the worldwide constituency for forest conservation both need reform. Neither category is airtight. For example, joint participation in financing policy reforms is greatly needed.

Policy Reforms by National Governments

Forestry Policies

Royalties and related charges on private concession holders in public timberlands have been deficient in two important ways. First, charges have been much less than the stumpage value of the timber. This has not only lost potential government revenue, but has also created enormous pressures from business and political interests to obtain timber concessions and the large rents they offer. Combined with other flaws in timber policy, this rent-seeking syndrome has led to over-rapid, wasteful exploitation, including the harvest of timber in critical watersheds and other ecologically vulnerable sites.

Second, in the developing countries, the structure of royalties has, usually in combination with inappropriate selection systems, exacerbated loggers' proclivities for high-grading forest stands and needlessly damaging remaining trees. Sensible reform calls both for sharp increases in many countries in royalty levels and for modification of defective royalty structures. Inflexible, undifferentiated, specific charges based on the volume of timber harvested should be replaced by differentiated *ad valorem* royalty systems based on export prices properly discounted for costs of harvesting logs and transporting them to ports, with lower rates for so-called ''secondary'' species than for the most valuable ''primary'' species. But, if their forest services are not sufficiently well-trained and administered to enforce such complex systems, flat-rate *ad valorem* royalties are second best, if set at moderate rates and combined with other measures to capture resource rents.

Governments have generally proven reluctant to enact royalty reform. Of the countries studied, only Sabah in 1978 and Liberia in 1979 have recently increased royalty levels sharply. China has sharply increased log prices administratively and by permitting market transactions, and proposals pending in China in 1987 will raise stumpage fees further. In Malaysia, the Philippines, Indonesia, Ivory Coast, Ghana, Gabon and elsewhere, royalties continue well below true stumpage values and should be raised. In the United States, although royalties are bid (usually competitively) and approximate private stumpage values, timber with negative stumpage values is routinely harvested because government absorbs substantial logging costs. The simplest remedy for this problem is the imposition of minimum acceptable bid prices high enough to recover the government's full separable costs of growing and marketing timber.

Inflexible, undifferentiated, specific charges based on the volume of timber harvested should be replaced by differentiated **ad valorem** *royalty systems based on export prices properly discounted for costs of harvesting logs and transporting them to ports, with lower rates for so-called ''secondary'' species than for the most valuable ''primary'' species.*

These changes would restrict harvesting of uneconomic forest lands, slow the pace of timber exploitation in Third World countries to match the growth of forest management capabilities, permit more complete utilization of the timber resources available in smaller, more compact concession areas, and thus reduce wastage, infrastructure costs, and the forest disturbance that opens the way for secondary clearance and agricultural conversion.

Reform of concessions policies also requires changes in duration of concessions and in the level of area license fees. Prior to the Second World War, many tropical timber concessions were granted for up to a century. Newly independent governments tended to view such arrangements as vestiges of colonialism, so the concession periods were steadily compressed. By 1987, concessions were typically for 5 to 10 years even for large tracts; few were longer than 20 years. Given the long growing cycles of tropical hardwoods, logging firms now have scant financial interest in maintaining forest productivity. Instead, they repeatedly reenter logged-over stands before their concessions expire, compounding damages from the initial harvest.

Foresters have advocated extending concession periods to at least 70 years, to provide loggers with two cutting cycles of 35 years each. Governments have ignored such proposals, partly because loggers practiced little conservation under longer pre-war concessions. Therefore, appropriate safeguards to defend the public interest must accompany extensions in concession periods. For example, concessionaire performance should be periodically reviewed, and logging rights renewed or extended only if licensees have adhered to prescribed practices: after a favorable five-year performance review, a 20- or 30- year concession could be extended for five more years, keeping the remaining period constant.

In practice, as Philippines' experience shows, such schemes are hard to police without better administrative capacity. Further, firms, especially multinational companies, have grown wary of long-term contracts, including timber concessions, because so many have been abrogated by host governments after internal political changes. A complementary approach is to structure incentives from the outset to induce firms to use forest resources rationally.

For example, governments can use area license fees much more effectively to promote conservation, rational harvesting, and more complete rent capture. Fees based on the area awarded in concessions have been extremely low in most countries. Ideally, logging concessions should be auctioned competitively, as offshore oil leases are in the United States, ensuring that governments capture virtually all the available resource rent. Auction or competitive bidding systems work well only if all parties have enough information about particular forest tracts to ascertain their approximate timber value. Getting this information is difficult since tropical forests are typically inaccessible and far more heterogeneous in species composition than temperate forests. Nevertheless, successful auction systems have been reported in Sarawak and Venezuela. The investment by governments in more detailed forest exploration and inventory is likely to have an immediate pay-off in improved revenue capture.

Auction systems can be combined with higher reservation or minimum bid prices to guard against bid-rigging or to discourage firms from entering ecologically sensitive regions or regions better reserved for harvesting at some future time. Where auction systems are not feasible, concession contracts should employ much higher license fees per hectare than is now common in the tropics. Higher license fees serve two conservation goals as well as revenue objectives: they discourage exploitation of stands of marginal commercial value, and, when combined with royalty systems differentiated with respect to stumpage values, they encourage economic utilization of timber stands by providing logging firms with incentives to harvest greater volume and more species per hectare.

Governments can use area license fees much more effectively to promote conservation, rational harvesting, and more complete rent capture.

In nearly all the countries studied, there have been serious problems with the selective harvesting systems that are used in almost all mixed tropical forests. Notwithstanding some evidence that careful selective logging can be done with minimal damage to residual stands, the selective cutting methods actually practiced in tropical forests yield unsatisfactory ecological results, principally because of heavy incidental damage, poor regeneration of harvested species, and inferior long-term economic results.

It is unfortunately true that while virtually no one supports clearcutting in tropical forests as a system for sustained natural forest management, no clear preference has yet been established for any selection system. There is therefore no basis for blanket prescriptions for changes in harvest methods. But, better enforcement of concession terms to avoid excess damage to soils and remaining trees is possible, and the policy reforms discussed above would provide stronger incentives to concessionaires to reduce logging damage and waste.

The most sensible long-run approach to improving harvest methods is to conduct more research on the ecological, silvicultural, and economic implications of alternative selection methods. The most plausible alternative to current methods is one or another of the so-called uniform cutting systems, which also involve selective harvests but generally take more stems per hectare. Uniform cutting systems involve greater short-term logging expenses but provide for a greater initial harvest and less wastage.

Reforestation in temperate forests is well understood, though costs and other constraints have sometimes limited reforestation programs on public lands. The situation is entirely different in tropical countries. Restoration of logged-over stands to something closely resembling their natural states with similar species frequency and density is difficult given existing knowledge of tropical forest ecology. Even enrichment planting of primary species in cut-over stands has encountered problems.

Facing these obstacles, some reforestation policies have mainly served other purposes. Indonesia's reforestation deposit (US$4 per cubic meter harvested) captured additional timber rents and helped discourage logging on marginal stands, but it has not induced firms to undertake significant reforestation activity. The principal incentive for concessionaires may be the opportunity to harvest completely the merchantable timber in natural forests before replanting. The same might be said of similar charges in Malaysia and West Africa. Nor have government regeneration programs had much success, whether financed by earmarked forest taxes or directly from national treasuries. Most of these programs have been either underbudgeted as in the Philippines, Ghana, and Gabon, ill-designed as in Indonesia and the Philippines, or have been rendered ineffective by institutional constraints, as in Sabah.

A viable set of regeneration policies in logged-over areas would include (1) selection systems favorable to natural regeneration, coupled with enrichment planting of native species; (2) carrot-and-stick incentives for firms to undertake regeneration; (3) more budgetary and scientific resources for regeneration research programs; and (4) more support for government regeneration efforts by international lending institutions.

Where reforestation is defined as replacement of forest cover on cut-over tracts by non-indigenous trees (such as pines) other than those grown for tree crops, some success has been recorded in tropical countries, including Indonesia, Malaysia, the Philippines, and Brazil although plantations of relatively low-valued species that have been established in concession areas far from potential markets have little

---

A viable set of regeneration policies in logged-over areas would include (1) selection systems favorable to natural regeneration, coupled with enrichment planting of native species; (2) carrot-and-stick incentives for firms to undertake regeneration; (3) more budgetary and scientific resources for regeneration research programs; and (4) more support for government regeneration efforts by international lending institutions.

economic value. Plantation programs, especially for conifers, are well established in China, the United States, and other temperate countries such as Chile.

Plantations are an essential part of any program to conserve natural tropical forests because they create an alternative source of supply to meet growing domestic demands. The area under tree plantations in the tropics has increased substantially since 1945. It grew to 11 million hectares (excluding China) by 1980, and is expected to double by the end of the century. [Spears(A) 1983.]

Policies that promote investment in tree plantations can help reduce demands on natural forests. A number of countries have adopted incentive programs, including tax benefits, concessionary credits, and guaranteed markets to stimulate private investment in plantations.

Plantations are an essential part of any program to conserve natural tropical forests because they create an alternative source of supply to meet growing domestic demands.

This study has not evaluated such policies because others have already done so in some detail. (Berger 1980; Evans 1984; Gregersen and McGauhey 1985; Laarman 1983; Matomoros 1982.) However, even with increasing investments in plantations, deforestation exceeds reforestation by large margins in most tropical countries, depletion of timber supplies greatly exceeds additions from all sources, and demands from export markets for high-valued tropical hardwoods cannot be met by plantation species. Consequently, positive incentives for plantation investments, while important, are insufficient. Adverse policies that exacerbate losses of natural forest resources must also be changed.

Neglect of non-timber forest products is one such adverse policy. Most tropical country governments do not even collect information on the annual value of production or export of dozens of valuable non-wood products that are harvested without damaging the forest ecosystem. Among the countries studied, only Indonesia keeps adequate data on these items, which now exceed 10 percent of gross log export value. Better information would be useful. If governments realize the value of such products, they will view their loss with more concern. Complicated new policies to protect non-timber products are not needed, but export taxes on them should be removed and export controls relaxed except, of course, for trade in sensitive or endangered species.

Traditionally, local communities have been more sensitive to these benefits, while central governments have tended to regard tropical forests as immense timber warehouses. Even then, central governments have not been effective resource managers, nor have provincial or state governments done much better. Transfer to private hands of permanent rights to natural forests is not a realistic option in most countries (both for constitutional and other reasons). In Brazil, where such transfers have taken place on a large scale, many large investors have been drawn to opportunities for short-term or speculative gains (in large part due to policy-induced distortions in investment incentives).

Experience does suggest that unambiguous local communal or collective ownership of forest property rights has been more consistent with conservation of all forest values than has central government ownership. Accordingly, a larger share of formal rights to natural forests should be returned to local jurisdictions, where long-standing traditions of forest use exist, to county governments (such as Indonesia's kabupatens) or to village cooperatives, as in China. Central governments would retain sovereign taxing power, and therefore would not give up forest revenues, though revenue-sharing with local communities is not only equitable but also effective in ensuring their interest in resource management. Reversion would mean principally that more decisions about forest management and land-clearing for agriculture would be in the hands of local groups with a continuing stake in the multiple benefits that natural forests provide.

Other Policies that Influence Forestry

Government policies have resulted in more resource depletion than would have occurred had governments tried to minimize their effects on private decisions over forest utilization. The point is not that laissez-faire would have been the desirable policy stance but that with market outcomes as a standard of comparison, government policies, on balance, have tended to encourage more rapid exploitation rather than more conservation. Economic policies affecting the forest sector have exacerbated deforestation in almost every country investigated. In several, these effects have been extremely large.

Income tax holidays for logging and processing firms have compounded the failure to collect adequate royalties and have fueled timber booms in the Philippines, Malaysia, and Indonesia. In Southeast Asia, most holidays have expired, but they are in force in Gabon, the Ivory Coast, and other African countries. These unnecessary holidays should be rescinded where they still survive. Other tax incentives, such as tax credits, accelerated depreciation, and other special deductions,

create perverse incentives for logging and forest-clearing, often making socially wasteful projects privately profitable. They too should be removed.

Credit subsidies have added to these perverse incentives. Artificially low interest rates and long grace periods on loans for ranching, estate crops, and other forest-clearing industries have proven irresistible (especially when coupled with generous tax subsidies), even when the industries were intrinsically uneconomic. All kinds of subsidized credit programs have proven wasteful. Credit subsidies for irreversible destruction of forest assets, unjustifiable on economic or environmental grounds, should be abolished.

Countries with forest endowments and low labor costs have a long-run comparative advantage in wood-processing industries. Govern-

ments in industrial countries where processing industries rely on imported logs have resisted this fact, erecting trade barriers against imported wood products and retaining capital and labor in declining industries. Governments in log-exporting countries have adopted policies to force exports of processed wood and to encourage investments in wood-based industries. Log export bans have led to smuggling, corruption, and the construction of high-cost processing facilities as a means of ensuring access to logs. Tax and tariff protection of wood-processing industries has been so high as to undermine incentives to minimize costs. These conflicting trade policies have distorted investment patterns and reduced economic efficiency, though tariffs also reduced world consumption of tropical timber somewhat. In some countries, billions of dollars in potential resource rents have been destroyed. Moreover, the resulting low recovery rates in timber processing have intensified demands on natural forest endowments.

Replacing log export quotas and bans with increased export taxes in countries with large wood-processing industries would increase government revenues and convince processing industries of the need to raise efficiency. This change should be negotiated internationally in exchange for lower barriers against processed-wood imports into industrial countries. The result should be a gradual transfer of most tropical wood processing to countries with large forest endowments, combined with substantial modernization and improved efficiencies.

The costly lesson of experience can still be put to good use in countries where forest-based industries have yet to emerge on a large scale (in East Malaysia, Gabon, Zaire, Cameroon, Papua New Guinea, and Burma, for example). The lesson is that gradual progress in forest-based industrialization wins over haste. Moderately higher export taxes on logs than on lumber and plywood are superior to bans or quotas on log exports. Export taxes furnish whatever protection is desired, raise government revenues, and also replace income tax or credit incentives for sawmills and plymills.

Large-scale resettlement programs that have moved people into forested regions have been based on the same wishful thinking that is behind ambitious forest-based industrialization. It has been wishful thinking that sponsored outmigration could relieve pressures of rural poverty, land scarcity, and environmental degradation in overcrowded areas. The costs of resettlement have been too high, and the numbers resettled too small to make such a strategy viable without dealing with the root problems of rapid population growth, rural inequality,

and underemployment in already settled areas. Similarly, those in need of resettlement (because displaced by large infrastructure projects, such as dams), have often been victims of wishful thinking that produced inflated estimates of projected returns on such investments. Most such investments have experienced serious cost and schedule overruns and have produced benefits only a fraction as large as anticipated.

The best guard against such over-optimism and the human, environmental, and economic losses it entails is to make the expected beneficiaries responsible for most of the costs of such projects. In all developing countries, spontaneous migrants outnumber government-sponsored migrants several fold and typically bear all their moving costs as an investment toward an anticipated better future for themselves and their offspring. If resettlement programs were based on the principle of cost recovery, the need for sound planning would be reinforced and there would be checks on the scale and pace of implementation. Similarly, if agencies responsible for large-scale development projects, such as dams, were financially responsible for recovering operating and most capital costs from project-generated revenues, inflated projections of investment returns would be brought down to earth. (Repetto 1986.)

Where resettlement programs are carried out, needless damage to natural forests can be reduced in several ways. The most obvious, of course, is not to locate new communities in natural forests at all. In many countries, ineffective or inappropriate land and agricultural tax policies allow large landholders to retain huge estates that are used to only a small fraction of their agricultural potential. In such countries, because smallholders typically achieve much higher per-hectare yields and incomes through intensive cultivation, land redistribution with compensation can be brought about, provided that the government is able to reform rural taxes to induce large landowners to sell part of their holdings and is willing to finance land purchases by small farmers on long-term mortgage credit.

In addition, degraded public forest lands and wastelands in many Third World countries could be transferred to landless peasants to be used for mixed farming systems involving agroforestry. The Chinese government has pursued this option vigorously in recent years. The main problem here is that government agencies are typically as reluctant to disgorge any of their estates as any other large landholder.

If any agricultural resettlement projects or plantations are sited in forest areas, logged-over and degraded tracts should be selected in preference to intact forests. Individual holdings must be large enough to allow sustained support so that settlers are not forced to encroach on adjacent forest areas. Colonies should be based largely on such tree crops as rubber, which are more suitable to available soils, and on agroforestry systems. Collection, storage, and marketing facilities for non-wood forest products near resettlement sites would encourage relocated families to use forests sustainably. Finally, award of sites must irrevocably convey all property rights to the awardee, including clear rights of transfer. This approach not only enables resettled peoples to offer land as collateral in borrowing for improvements, but also reinforces the incentive to protect and enhance value of the property.

This discussion of domestic policy options cannot be completed without drawing attention to the connection between deforestation and failed development policies. Pressures on natural forests are reduced when towns and villages achieve adequate growth in rural output and employment, begin to convert from wood as an energy source to electricity and petroleum products, and experience declining population growth rates as birth and death rates decline and young workers are drawn off into expanding urban industries. By contrast, economic stagnation and poverty inevitably accelerate deforestation.

Not much is known about government policies that accelerate economic development, except those that promote a stable, broadly based political and economic system and reward enterprise and productive investment by households and businesses. Much painful experience has accumulated, however, about economic policies that retard development.

Among these are deeply overvalued exchange rates, negative interest rates, and flagrantly distorted commodity prices. These result in serious market disequilibria, scarcities, and rationing throughout the economy. They also create perverse investment incentives and generate speculation and corruption. Such policies also often imply heavy penalties on the rural sector, as the prices of agricultural outputs are lowered relative to industrial prices and investments are redirected toward the urban sector. If, at the same time, governments expand their direct role in the economy beyond their managerial capabilities, creating expensive state-operated industrial and agricultural white elephants, economic stagnation is nearly assured.

Reversal of policies clearly inimical to growth will not immediately stem the spread of shifting cultivation and the search for fuelwood. But the recent experiences of such relatively prosperous countries as Gabon, Venezuela, and the western part of Malaysia reveal little deforestation arising from either shifting cultivation or fuelwood demands.

Policy Changes by Industrial Countries and International Agencies

Of course, economic development in tropical countries is influenced by industrial countries' policies. Much of the Third World has suffered stagnation and decline in the 1980s as a consequence of worldwide recession in the early 1980s, high real interest rates, sharp reductions in net capital flows to developing countries, and trade protection in the industrial countries. The connection must be pointed out between economic stagnation leading to deforestation in the Third World and policies in industrial countries that restrict capital flows to developing countries and markets for developing country exports.

More specifically, industrial-country trade barriers in the forest products sector have been partially responsible for inappropriate investments and patterns of exploitation in Third World forest industries. Whether within the context of the General Agreement on Tariffs and Trade (GATT), the International Tropical Timber Agreement (ITTA), or some other international forum, negotiations between exporting and importing countries should reduce tariff escalation and non-tariff barriers to processed wood imports from the tropical countries, and rationalize incentives to forest industries in the Third World.

While international assistance agencies have become increasingly concerned with forest sector problems over the past 15 years, their involvement has primarily been support for discrete development projects. These have ranged widely, from reforestation and watershed rehabilitation projects to support for fuelwood and industrial timber plantations and to funding for wood processing industries.

Industrial-country trade barriers in the forest products sector have been partially responsible for inappropriate investments and patterns of exploitation in Third World forest industries.

Associated with them, of course, has been a significant amount of technical assistance in a wide variety of forestry-related subjects.

It must also be said that development assistance agencies have, in the aggregate, provided huge amounts of funding for projects that lead directly and indirectly to deforestation, including roads, dams, tree crop plantations, and agricultural settlements. Greater sensitivity is required in ensuring that such projects are, wherever possible, sited away from intact forests and especially away from critical ecosystems; that such investments are, in fact, economically and ecologically sound if forest losses are weighed in the balance; and that projects are executed with effective safeguards to minimize unnecessary damages.

Only to a much lesser extent have development assistance agencies been involved with the kinds of sectoral policy issues discussed in this book. The Food and Agriculture Organization of the United Nations (FAO) has indeed studied forest revenue systems and published manuals and related material for policymakers. Multilateral and bilateral assistance agencies such as the Inter-American Development Bank and USAID have examined policies that would encourage private investment in forestry. In recent years, the World Bank has carried out forest sector reviews in several countries that address some of the broader policy issues identified in this report and new directions in World Bank policies indicate growing attention to tropical forests. Yet, still more emphasis on policy reform in the forest sector is required. Especially as international capital flows become increasingly divorced from specific projects and linked to broad macroeconomic and sectoral policy agreements, the international development agencies must identify and analyze the effects of tax, tariff, credit, and pricing policies, as well as the terms and administration of concession agreements, on the use of forest resources. Cooperating with host country agencies, they can do more to identify needs for policy changes and options for policy reform.

More generally, governments of industrialized countries and international agencies should act upon the recognized community of interests among all nations in the conservation of tropical forests. During 1987 the FAO, the World Bank, the United Nations Development Programme, and the World Resources Institute collaborated with non-government organizations, professional associations, and governments around the world on a "tropical forestry action plan." (FAO 1987.) Intended not as a blueprint but as a framework for coordinated action, this plan identifies priority action needed on five fronts: forest-related land uses; forest-based industrial development; fuelwood and energy; conservation of tropical forest ecosystems; and institution-building. Its recommendations complement the policy changes outlined in this study.

The call for action sounded by participants in the process that led to the action plan serves equally well as a conclusion to this report: "Above all, action is needed now. Hundreds of millions of people in developing countries already face starvation because of fuel and food shortages. The forest resource potential of these countries can and must be harnessed to meet their development needs. Properly used and managed, the tropical forests constitute massive potential sources of energy, a powerful tool in the fight to end hunger, a strong basis for generating economic wealth and social development, and a storehouse of genetic resources to meet future needs. This is the promise and the challenge."

Still more emphasis on policy reform in the forest sector is required. Especially as international capital flows become increasingly divorced from specific projects and linked to broad macroeconomic and sector policy agreements, the international development agencies must identify and analyze the effects of tax, tariff, credit, and pricing policies.

It is by no means too late. Although in many countries, such as El Salvador, Haiti, Liberia, the Ivory Coast, and the Philippines, the natural forest has been extensively disturbed or virtually destroyed, in others—Brazil and Indonesia, for example—huge forests remain, and in still other countries, such as Gabon, the Congo, and Zaire, most forests are still untouched. In some of these countries, inaccessibility rather than policy effectively but only temporarily restrains the timber harvest. The Transgabonnais Highway is opening up new large areas of virgin forests even while still under construction, for example. Enacting rational policies toward forest exploitation, forest-based industrialization, and conversion of forests to other land uses will conserve these important resources and forestall serious economic and fiscal losses.

Notes

1. A standing tree's stumpage value is its implicit market worth, estimated by subtracting from the market value of the wood products that can be derived from it all the costs of harvesting, transporting to mill, and processing.

2. Ironically, Ghana, where forestry administration has been relatively weak, operates an

effectively differentiated system of specific royalties. A different royalty rate applies to each of 39 commercial species, and rates are charged per tree (rather than per cubic meter) harvested. This system encourages loggers to harvest a variety of species, to harvest large trees and thereby open the forest canopy for regeneration, and to utilize each stem cut as fully as possible. Unfortunately, since Ghana has almost no virgin production forests left,

these beneficial effects cannot be fully realized there.

3. A loan that has a negative real interest rate is one on which the nominal rate of interest charged is less than the trend rate of inflation. With such a loan, the borrower could invest in any asset appreciating at the rate of inflation, sell it when the loan is due, repay the loan with interest, and make a profit.

II. Country Studies

Indonesia

Estimates of Indonesia's forest area in 1985 range from 143 to 157 million hectares, roughly three-quarters of the total land area. On 64 to 68 million hectares of production forest—nearly 60 percent of the productive forest area in Southeast Asia—commercial timber harvesting is legally and physically possible. This is nearly 60 percent of the productive forest area in Southeast Asia. About 40 percent of the country is covered by tropical rain forests, mostly in Kalimantan (Indonesian Borneo), Sumatra and West Irian. Because trees of the prized *Dipterocarpaceae* family predominate (Ashton 1984), Indonesia may have the world's most valuable tropical rain forest.

Degradation and disappearance of Indonesian forests have accelerated since 1967. Estimated annual deforestation has increased to 700,000 hectares in 1985, by far the highest in Southeast Asia. Most deforestation stems from land clearance for agriculture, but commercial timber production levels also increased through 1983. *(See Table II.A.1).*

The timber boom of the 1970s stemmed from policies adopted by the new Suharto government in 1967. Faced with severe economic problems and viewing the country's forests as a ready revenue source, the new regime awarded generous timber concessions to foreign companies eager to exploit vast, untapped stands of valuable tropical hardwoods. Five-year income tax holidays, which some companies were able to extend for up to 15 years, nearly doubled their after-tax investment returns. Fiscal losses from income tax holidays, which may have been as much as US$2 billion since 1967, was only one of the ways the Indonesian government sacrificed timber revenues. From 1979 to 1982, the forest revenue system collected only US$1.6 billion of a potential aggregate rent of US$4.4 billion. The remaining US$2.8 billion was left as private profit or absorbed in pay-offs to various authorities. (P.T. Data Consult 1983: 18-37).

Estimated annual deforestation in Indonesia has increased to 700,000 hectares in 1985, by far the highest in Southeast Asia.

These financial interests created strong pressures to expand the concession area beyond the government's ability to administer and supervise agreements. By 1983, concessions had been granted on 65.4 million hectares—more than the total area of Indonesia's productive forests.

The timber boom's effects on Indonesia's forests were compounded by structural flaws in royalty and license fees, concession durations,

43

Table II.A.1. Indonesia: Physical Volume of Log Harvest and Export Values of Tropical Timber 1960–87

Year	Total Log Harvest million of m³	All Timber Product	Logs only
1960–65 average	2.5	n.a.	n.a.
1970	10.0	110	110
1975	16.3	527	527
1976	21.4	885	885
1977	22.2	943	943
1978	24.2	1,130	1,052
1979	25.3	2,172	2,060
1980	25.2	1,672	1,428
1981	15.9	951	504
1982	13.4	899	310
1983	14.9	1,161	267
1984	16.1	1,120	178
1985	24.3	1,185	44
1986	25.0[a]	1,376	1
1987	26.0[a]	n.a.	n.a.

Source: For 1960–85: Department Kehutanan 1984; For 1986–87: Ministry of Finance.

Notes: Export values are for fiscal years i.e. 1975 = 1975/76. The fiscal year ends on March 30. It is to be noted that different sources provide rather different estimates of the total annual harvest of logs by year, often differing by as much as 2 million cubic meters per year. The figures provided in the first column are taken from the most widely used sources.

[a]preliminary

n.a. not available

and harvesting systems. Current guidelines of the Indonesian Selective Logging System (ISLS) limit harvests to the large stems of commercially valuable species [Spears(B) 1983], only a fraction of the potentially marketable timber. Consequently, larger forest areas must be logged to obtain any desired output than under more uniform cutting systems.

Basing royalties on removals rather than on the volume of merchantable trees in a stand also encourages concessionaires to harvest only the most valuable stems. Also, since the royalty is a flat *ad valorem* rate, with no distinction for species, grade, or size, loggers have little incentive to protect immature, inferior, or less marketable varieties with little after-tax stumpage value if they can reduce the costs of extracting higher-value stems. Nearly 40 percent of the stems not removed are so severely affected that they perish before the next cutting. Heavy damage is inflicted on new saplings and seedlings, decreasing the probability of regeneration. Short concession periods averaging only 20 years, much less than optimal rotation periods, further weaken incentives for sustained yield management. Commonly, loggers have reentered stands and

*From 1979 to 1982, the Indonesian
forest revenue system collected only
US$1.6 billion of a potential aggregate
rent of US$4.4 billion. The remaining
US$2.8 billion was left as private profit
or absorbed in pay-offs to various
authorities.*

stripped them of remaining timber before adequate recovery or regeneration, with little
attempt to control damage.

Enforcement of the ISLS and concession
terms has been poor too. There are few government agents to monitor the vast forests, or
to police harvesting practices in remote concession areas. Furthermore, high potential rents
have promoted corruption. As a result, private
firms have avoided regulations, increasing their
profits at the forest's expense.

Forest-Based Industrialization

Government policies beyond the Forestry
Department's jurisdiction have also affected
forest exploitation drastically in recent years.
Since the 1970s, policies have promoted
domestic forest-based industries. In 1978, the
ad valorem export tax on logs was doubled from
10 percent to 20 percent while most sawnwood
and all plywood were exempted; in 1980, log
exports were progressively restricted until
totally banned in 1985. These policies stimulated rapid growth in the number of operating
and planned plymills from 16 in 1977 to 182 in
1983 (P.T. Data Consult 1983: 18-30), but many
were inefficient operations.

Harvests were initially reduced because log
exports fell before plymills had the capacity to
absorb excess log supplies. Recorded harvests
declined from their peak of 25 million cubic

meters in 1979 to 13 million cubic meters in
1982, and recovered to 16 million by 1986, but
alternative estimates suggest an actual harvest
near 25 million. Plymills will require 20 million
cubic meters of log feedstock by 1988, and sawmills will require 18 million cubic meters more,
a total of roughly 38 million cubic meters of
logs. Of this, only 1.3 million cubic meters will
be available from plantations, and natural
forests will have to provide the remaining 36.7
million cubic meters—almost 1.5 times more
than the previous peak in 1979. Furthermore,
government estimates for the next decade project continuing growth, to a harvest level in
1998 of three times the 1979 peak. (Department
of Kehutanan 1985.) Whether Indonesia's natural forests can sustain these harvests economically, and whether world markets can absorb
the output without declining prices, are sharply debated.

Indonesia's average conversion rates for
sawnwood (1.8 cubic meters log input per
cubic meter of output) and plywood (2.3 cubic
meters log input per cubic meter of output) are
among the least efficient in Asia. Plywood
production in Indonesia requires 15 percent
more logs per cubic meter of output than elsewhere in the region—a large difference at the
production levels projected for the 1990s.

Inefficient conversion, partly the result of the
government's generous protection to the industry, also has high costs. In plywood manufacturing, the value per cubic meter of product in
roundwood equivalent was only US$109 in
1983, when exported logs were worth US$100
per cubic meter. Local processing earned only
US$9 per cubic meter of logs used for ply-
wood, but the government lost US$20 in
potential export taxes. In 1983, since sawn
wood brought only US$85 per cubic meter in
roundwood equivalent, the government sacrificed US$20 per cubic meter of taxes from
unprocessed log exports only to *lose* US$15 in
foreign exchange earnings. Without protection
and government incentives to cover processing
costs, the industry could not have developed
so rapidly.

By 1988, there will be an estimated 150,000 jobs in plymills, which will require the harvest from an additional 800,000 hectares per year. Between 1988 and 1998, 8 million hectares of virgin forest will be logged, an area equal to 12.5 percent of the country's remaining productive forests and more than 53 hectares for each new job. The rapid expansion of relatively inefficient mills has heightened log demand, which is protected against market forces even as Indonesia's share in world plywood export markets increases.

Whether Indonesia's natural forests can sustain heavy harvests economically, and whether world markets can absorb the output without declining prices, are sharply debated.

Timber exploitation has hidden opportunity costs. As forests disappear, so do such valuable products as rattan, resin, sandalwood, meat, honey, natural silk, and pharmaceutical and cosmetic compounds, which can be harvested sustainably from tropical forests and exported. In 1982, these non-wood forest products brought in $120 million despite little government attention, more than the export values of copper, aluminum, tea, pepper, and tobacco. Most of the $120 million created income and employment in local economies, while much of the export value of wood products and logs is retained by timber companies as profit. Yet, government continues to consider wood the primary forest resource.

Forest degradation may also leave the ecosystem more vulnerable to such natural disasters as fires. In 1983, the most extensive fire ever recorded anywhere swept across Kalimantan and devastated an area the size of Belgium. Damage was most severe in logged-over regions because the dead wood and litter left after harvesting ignited readily. Virgin forests were not significantly affected. (Mackie 1984.)

Between 1988 and 1998, 8 million hectares of virgin forest will be logged, an area equal to 12.5 percent of Indonesia's remaining productive forests and more than 53 hectares for each new job created.

Rent Capture

The government's failure to capture available rents from timber harvesters has clearly driven the timber boom, which in turn has opened large areas for subsequent agricultural conversion. Potential rents per cubic meter of roundwood equivalent for logs, sawnwood, and plywood from 1979 to 1983 are shown in Table II.A.2. Potential rents from unprocessed logs were higher than those from sawn timber and plywood, except in 1979. Rents from plywood production were repeatedly negative after 1979, implying that costs exceeded economic returns.

Revenues from royalties, property and export taxes, and reforestation fees, were consistently less than 20 percent of exports through 1978. From that point, they increased gradually to roughly 37 percent in 1982, in response to the doubling of the export tax on logs in 1978. Table II.A.3 combines information on revenues and actual rents to provide estimates of the Indonesian government's effectiveness in capturing rents from 1979 to 1982. The percent of rent capture on log exports increased to 55 percent by 1982, while the percent on sawn timber rose to 46 percent. However, the average capture for logs was only half of that available (US$31 of a possible US$61 per cubic meter).

Table II.A.2. Indonesia: Hypothetical Rent per m³ of Roundwood Equivalent Tropical Timber 1979–83 US$ per m³

Year	(1) Average f.o.b. value per m³ of product US$	(2) Average f.o.b. value per m³ of Roundwood Equivalent US$	(3) Logging and Transport costs (to port) per m³ of Roundwood Equivalent US$	(4) Milling Costs per m³ of Roundwood Equivalent US$	(5) Potential Rent per m³ of Roundwood Equivalent Col. 2 minus (3+4)
1979					
[a]Logs	85.21	85.21	29.84	n.a.	55.37
[b]Sawnwood	183.42	100.78	29.84	10.36	60.58
[c]Plywood	271.11	117.87	29.84	56.48	31.55
1980					
[a]Logs	106.93	106.93	34.24	n.a.	72.69
[b]Sawnwood	214.55	117.24	34.24	11.92	71.08
[c]Plywood	227.49	98.90	34.24	64.93	−0.27
1981					
[a]Logs	95.84	95.84	37.93	n.a.	57.91
[b]Sawnwood	175.31	96.32	37.93	13.21	45.18
[c]Plywood	195.23	84.88	37.93	71.99	−25.04
1982					
[a]Logs	100.59	100.59	41.00	n.a.	59.59
[b]Sawnwood	150.78	82.84	41.00	14.28	27.56
[c]Plywood	229.12	99.61	41.00	77.82	−19.21
1983					
[a]Logs	99.10	99.10	45.92	n.a.	53.18
[b]Sawnwood	154.70	85.00	45.92	16.00	23.08
[c]Plywood	250.63	108.97	45.92	87.16	−24.11

Table II.A.2. Continued

Notes:

a. All timber products are valued at opportunity costs (world prices).
b. Conversion factors are: *sawnwood* − 1.82 m³ of logs for each m³ of sawnwood; *plywood* 2.3 m³ of logs for each m³ of plywood. Source: Department Kehutanan 1984. Source for Export Values: Department Kehutanan 1984. Source for Cost Data: Based on information from Hunter 1984: 109–110, and corroborated by cost data in P.T. Data Consult 1983: 9.

Hunter's figure for logging plus transport cost to mills for 1982 was US$35.00 (average for East Kalimantan, source of 21 percent of Indonesia's timber exports). This figure does not, apparently, include harbor fees and associated export costs of approximately US$2.00 per cubic meter. Further, an estimate by Buenaflor (cited in Beer and Rossini) for logging costs indicates such costs at US$44.60 per cubic meter in 1980. In view of the discrepancies in estimates, a figure of US$41.00 per cubic meter was employed for logging/transport costs in 1982.

For other years, costs were assumed to rise as follows: one-half of costs rose pari-passu with world inflation; one-half rose pari-passu with domestic inflation (wholesale price index for manufactures). From 1979 to 1981, the rupiahs' nominal value was fixed at 630 per US$1.00, so costs were estimated as follows, per unit of product:

Cost in Logging and Milling by Product (per m³) US$

	1979	1980	1981	1982	1983
Logging and log transport costs per m³ of logs	29.84	34.24	37.93	41.00	45.92
Milling costs (Sawnwood)	18.86	21.69	24.05	26.00	29.12
Milling costs (Plywood)	129.91	149.34	165.58	179.00	200.48

In roundwood equivalents, using standard Indonesian conversion ratios (1.82 for sawntimber and 2.3 for plywood) milling costs results are presented below:

Milling Costs in Roundwood Equivalents (US$ per m³)

	1979	1980	1981	1982	1983
Milling costs (Sawnwood)	10.36	11.92	13.21	14.28	16.00
Milling costs (Plywood)	56.48	64.93	71.99	77.82	87.16

Table II.A.3. Estimated Timber Rent Capture by Government: Kalimantan and Sumatra 1979–82 Exclusive of Income Taxes (US$ per m³)

| | Rent Capture by Government m³ of Roundwood Equivalent | | |
	US Potential Rent per m³ [a]in Roundwood Equivalent	Timber Royalty (6% of f.o.b. Log Value at Export Point[b])	Timber Export Tax (20% for logs)
Year	(1)	(2)	(3)
1979			
[a]Logs	55.37	5.11	17.04
[b]Sawnwood	60.58	5.11	n.a.
[c]Plywood	31.55	5.11	n.a.
1980			
[a]Logs	72.69	6.41	21.39
[b]Sawnwood	71.08	6.41	n.a.
[c]Plywood	−0.27	6.41	n.a.
1981			
[a]Logs	57.91	5.75	19.17
[b]Sawnwood	45.18	5.75	n.a.
[c]Plywood	−25.04	5.75	n.a.
1982			
[a]Logs	59.59	6.03	20.12
[b]Sawnwood	27.56	6.03	n.a.
[c]Plywood	−19.21	6.03	n.a.

For sawnwood, of an average potential rent of US$51, only US$10 (i.e. twenty percent) was collected. As Table III.A.4 shows, aggregate rents from 1979 to 1982 fell by about a billion dollars per year because of the drop in log harvests and the increasing dissipation of rents in processing.

Table II.A.5 compares government's total forest revenue collection with the actual rent over the period 1979 to 1982, and also with the hypothetical potential rent that would have been generated had the entire log harvest been exported without processing. The difference

between hypothetical and actual rent, over US$545 million dollars, is one measure of the cost of inefficient processing operations. Close to US$2.8 billion was lost to excess profits and unauthorized payments over these four years, and another US$0.5 billion was lost in inefficient processing.

Other studies support the conclusion that Indonesian government promotion of domestic timber processing greatly reduced the potential rent base. Fitzgerald (1986) reported a net loss of roughly US$1 billion in plywood exports at prices below the cost of production.

Table II.A.3. Continued

| | Rent Capture by Government per m³ of Roundwood Equivalent | | | |
	Replanting Fee ($4.00 per m³)ᶜ	Other Levies Ipeda, the "Additional" Royalty	Total Rent Capture by Govt. (2+3+4+5)	Percent of Rent Captured by Govt. (6) – (1)
Year	**(4)**	**(5)**	**(6)**	**(7)**
1979				
ᵃLogs	n.a.	2.52	24.67	44.6
ᵇSawntimber	n.a.	2.52	7.63	12.6
ᶜPlywood	n.a.	2.52	7.63	24.2
1980				
ᵃLogs	n.a.	2.78	30.58	42.1
ᵇSawntimber	n.a.	2.78	9.19	12.9
ᶜPlywood	n.a.	2.78	9.19	–
1981				
ᵃLogs	4.00	2.65	31.57	54.5
ᵇSawntimber	4.00	2.65	12.40	27.5
ᶜPlywood	4.00	2.65	12.40	–
1982				
ᵃLogs	4.00	2.71	32.86	55.1
ᵇSawntimber	4.00	2.71	12.74	46.2
ᶜPlywood	4.00	2.71	12.74	–

Notes:

n.a. not applicable

a. Derived from Table II.A.2 (Potential Rent per m³).

b. Timber royalty structure was changed in July 1979. Since then, a 6-percent *ad valorem* rate has applied to the f.o.b. value of all timber produced by concession holders. The 6 percent royalty applies to the "check price" (posted price), which since 1972 has ordinarily been 5 to 9 percent below actual export values. The estimates in this table apply to values in round-wood equivalent at the check price, and thus understate rents by perhaps 5 to 10 percent per year.

c. Replanting fee enacted in 1981; imposed on log production in Kalimantan and Sumatra.

Transmigration

Public policy since the early 1900s has been to move large numbers of people from the densely settled islands of Java, Bali, and Madura to the sparsely populated Outer Islands so as to relieve pressure on over-stressed watersheds and to open new land for agriculture. By 1985, at least 2.5 million people had been relocated, and a larger number migrated without govern-

Table II.A.4. Aggregate Rents in Tropical Timber: Logs, Sawnwood and Plywood US$ Millions 1979–82

	LOGS		
	Logs not Utilized in Sawnwood and Plywood million m³	Logs Rent per m³ US$	Aggregate Rent in Logging US$ (A) × (B) millions
Year	(A)	(B)	(C)
1979	21.24	55.37	1,176.1
1980	20.77	72.69	1,509.8
1981	10.89	57.91	630.6
1982	7.43	59.59	442.8

	SAWNWOOD		
	Production million m³ of Roundwood Equivalent	Rent per m³ of Roundwood Equivalent US$	Aggregate Rent in Sawnwood millions US$ (D) × (E)
	(D)	(E)	(F)
1979	3.50	60.58	212.0
1980	3.41	71.08	242.4
1981	3.51	45.18	158.6
1982	3.75	27.56	103.3

	PLYWOOD		
	Production million m³ of Roundwood Equivalent	Rent per m³ US$	Aggregate Rent in Plywood US$ (G) × (H)	Total Rent: (C) + (F) + (I) US$ mil.
	(G)	(H)	(I)	(J)
1979	0.47	31.55	14.8	1,402.9
1980	1.01	−0.27	−0.3	1,751.9
1981	1.55	−25.04	−38.8	750.4
1982	2.20	−19.21	−42.3	503.8

ment support. Official estimates place the cost of relocating a family at nearly US$10,000. In 1984, the program accounted for 2.9 percent of federal development expenditures, more than the share of all public health and family planning programs. (Ross 1984: 57; Ross 1982: 94.)

Transmigration programs have had severe environmental consequences. Soils underlying most of the undisturbed forests are not particularly fertile. When settlements are improperly sited, or when an area is improperly cleared, soil fertility declines as remaining nutrients are

Table II.A.5. Government Share in Actual and Hypothetical Timber Rents 1979–82

	(1) Total Hypothetical Rents US$ mil.	(2) Total Actual Rents US$ mil.	(3) Govt. Tax Collection on Timber US$ mil.	(4) Govt. Share Hypothetical Rents (1) ÷ (3)	(5) Govt. Share Hypothetical Rents (2) ÷ (3)
1979	1,401.6	1,402.9	488.6	34.9	34.8
1980	1,831.1	1,751.9	542.5	29.6	31.0
1981	923.9	750.4	351.9	38.1	46.9
1982	797.1	503.8	261.1	32.7	51.8
TOTAL	4,953.7	4,409.0	1,644.1	33.2	37.3

scraped off or leach out. Very few transmigration sites have sustained agricultural yields high enough to support the resettled population for long. These problems and frequent managerial breakdowns have caused the clearing of additional acreage beyond original boundaries. (Setyono, Haerum, Sibero and Ross 1985: 64–65.) Even successful relocations have triggered additional deforestation when migrants ignorant of farming techniques suitable for local conditions spontaneously move in to share the prosperity. (Secrett 1986: 77–85.)

In the 1980s, economic and environmental costs forced a reduction in the transmigration program. Indonesia's government also now plans to place 80 percent of future transmigrants in rubber and other commercial tree-cropping projects so that areas unsuited for annual crops can be settled and environmental problems associated with earlier settlements reduced.

If current plans to relocate an additional 15 million people by the year 2000 materialize, an estimated 12 million hectares of presently forested land would be cleared. A more promising alternative would be to site transmigration projects on degraded forest lands after they are rehabilitated.

Malaysia

Malaysia is divided into three distinct regions: Peninsular Malaysia, encompassing twelve states, and the states of Sabah and Sarawak in northern Borneo. Forest endowments vary greatly between these areas, and state governments are largely autonomous in managing lands and forests.

Although regional forest policies are more important than national in Malaysia, a few generalizations are useful. Forest reserves in Malaysia covered about 60 percent, or 20.4 million hectares, of the total land area in 1981. Deforestation has increased, especially over the last decade, to an annual rate of more than 250,000 hectares per year by 1985. (*See Table I.B.1.*) These losses are 1.2 percent of total forested lands annually, more than twice the average reported for other tropical nations.

Sabah

Sabah, the smallest of the three regions, has 4.7 million hectares of forests in its total 7.4 million hectare land area. About 2 million hectares are undisturbed *Dipterocarp* forests, with potential commercial yields as high as 140

Table II.B.1. Malaysia: Total Annual Deforestation Due to All Causes 1975–85 (thousand hectares)

	Annual Deforestation Rate		Deforestation as % of Forest Area in 1981	
	1976–80	1980–85	1976–80	1980–85
I. Total Malaysia	230	255	0.011	0.125
II. Sabah	60	76	0.013	0.017
III. Sarawak	80	89	0.009	0.010
IV. Peninsular Malaysia	90	90	0.014	0.014

Sources: FAO 1981a: 289–290, 308–309, 326–327.

Table II.B.2. Sabah: Utilization of the Tropical Forest Estate: Deforestation Due to Shifting Cultivation, Area Utilized for Logging End 1980 (thousands of hectares)

I. Logged-over Forest (Stock)	1,280
II. Unlogged Natural Forest Under Logging License (Stock)	2,029
A. Under Regular Concession (21-year lease)	869
B. Under Special License (10-year lease)	782
C. Under Form I License (one-year lease)	77
D. Licenses Pending	301
III. Area Affected by Shifting Cultivation (Stock) (1970–1980 only)	3,650
IV. Annual Deforestation Rate Due to Shifting Cultivation (Flow)	
A. 1975–1980	36
B. 1980–1985	42
V. Annual Deforestation Rate Due to Logging and Conversion of Land to Permanent Agriculture	
A. 1976–1980	24
B. 1980–1985	34

Source: FAO 1981a: 301–309

cubic meters per hectare, though actual recoveries have been about half of that for large-scale loggers and one quarter of that for smaller operations. By 1980, 3.2 million hectares—essentially all of Sabah's productive forests—had already been logged or placed under logging concessions. [FAO 1981(A): 35, 297-305].

Since 1976, logging followed by agricultural conversion has accounted for between 40 and 45 percent of Sabah's deforestation. Shifting cultivation has been responsible for more than half of the state's annual forest loss. The total area affected by shifting cultivation amounted to three times the area of forest logged through 1980. *(See Table II.B.2.)*

Under laws dating from British Colonial rule, any citizen can gain title to forested land by clearing and working it, so as logging opened up previously inaccessible sites, indigenous people have followed, cleared the remaining forests, and claimed the land. Rural poverty, which affected more than 50 percent of the population in 1982, has encouraged this practice. (Segal 1983: 46.)

Benefits from Forest Exploitation

Sabah has been comparatively effective in capturing benefits from its forests. The timber industry, mainly logging, has provided roughly one third of the state's gross regional product since 1970 and 7 percent of total employment in the late 1970s, a level several times higher than in Peninsular Malaysia or Indonesia. Timber exports tripled in value from 1971 to 1976, and doubled again from 1977 to 1982, when logs and sawnwood averaged 41 percent of the state's gross exports.

Since 1970, forest-based taxes and royalties have ranged from one half to two thirds of total revenues, peaking at 71 percent in 1980. (Chong 1980: 42.) Royalties (accounting for 80 to 90 percent of total timber receipts) were consistently a much higher percentage of gross export values than in other South Eastern Asian countries. For instance, forest revenues in Sabah increased from 26 percent of total exports in 1974 to 60 percent in 1980—a level nearly double that in Indonesia. (Gillis 1980.)

Forestry Policies

Given the richness and accessibility of many of Sabah's hardwood stands, it is not surprising that the timber royalty is the highest anywhere in the world, as shown in Table II.B.3. The charges are designed so that the government's share increases with world log prices. (See Table II.B.3). After the export tax on logs was doubled in Indonesia in 1978, the Sabah royalty was raised from a maximum of 36 percent to a maximum of 57 percent of export values. Its average yield since 1979 has been 54 percent.

These charges have clearly provided critical revenue for the state government, but have added to pressures on Sabah's forests since they are *ad valorem* charges based on *gross* export value and royalties rise as log prices increase. Such charges promote high-grading, so a larger area must be logged to obtain the same harvest. High-grading is evident in Sabah, since recovery rates are only 25-50 percent of the potential yield. [FAO 1981(A): 301].

The state's concession system has compounded these consequences. Three types of concessions, lasting from one to 25 years, have been offered to timber firms in Sabah. Unfortunately, 50 percent of all concessions granted by 1980 lasted only one or five years, so harvesters had no incentives to use techniques that reduce damage, help to sustain yield, or preserve the productive and protective function of the forest. As a result, 72 percent of uncut trees are damaged by logging in Sabah, while 42 percent are affected under the more benign system used in Sarawak. Furthermore, the proportion of broken or missing trees in logged-over stands in Sabah is nearly 62 percent, compared to only 14.6 percent in Sarawak.

Extensive and wasteful logging may have left Sabah's forests more susceptible to the fires that swept over millions of hectares in Sabah and Indonesia in 1983. Logged-over areas with much combustible litter suffered tremendous damage, while unlogged forests escaped.

Forest-Based Industrialization

The policy devices that Sabah's government has used to stimulate a domestic forest-based industry were applied later and less aggressively than in Indonesia. Log export restrictions, not adopted until 1979 and leniently applied since then, have had less effect in developing the wood products industry than strict enforcement of heavy royalties and taxes. At an f.o.b. value of US$100 per cubic meter, close to actual prices in the early 1980s, royalties would be US$51.56 per cubic meter for

Table II.B.3. Comparison of Approximate Timber Royalty Payments Per Cubic Meter at Various f.o.b. Prices for Meranti Logs: Sabah, Sarawak and Indonesia

| Country | f.o.b. Log Prices (US$ millions) | | | |
	$75	$100	$125	$150
Sabah	33.39	48.39	66.92	84.82
Sarawak (Pre-1980)	5.53	5.53	5.53	5.53
Sarawak (Post-1980)	9.25	9.25	9.25	9.25
Indonesia (Basic and additional royalty)	6.00	7.50	9.00	10.50

unprocessed logs versus only US$7 per cubic meter for those processed locally. The difference of US$44.56 per cubic meter between these figures strongly encourages sawmilling, to take advantage of Sabah's dense and uniformly low-quality hardwood stands. Royalties

---

Fifty percent of all concessions granted in Sabah by 1980 lasted only one or five years, so harvesters had no incentives to use techniques that reduce damage, help to sustain yield, or preserve the productive and protective function of the forest.

---

provided strong incentives for investment in sawmills after 1979, although incentives were weakened in 1983 by a new tax on sawn timber.

In terms of equivalent roundwood, f.o.b. values for sawnwood around 1980 were not more than 122 percent of log prices. In 1980, the government thus sacrificed US$44.56 in royalties per cubic meter of logs milled domestically for every US$22 gained in value-added. The revenue lost, 200 percent of the incremental value-added, represents sawmills' rate of

effective protection. The effective rate declined to 146 percent in 1982 when a new export tax on sawn timber of US$8 per cubic meter was imposed.

The number of sawmills consequently jumped from only 12 before 1978 to more than 200 by 1981, but nearly one third of them closed in response to the tax on sawnwood in 1983. When sawmill capacity can absorb the log harvest, about 30,000 workers—6 percent of the 1986 labor force—will be employed in the mills and 7 percent more in logging. There will be substantial pressure to maintain harvests to keep mills open even in times of low global demand.

Rent Capture

Estimates of logging and sawmilling costs for Sabah are varied, but on average are probably close to Indonesia's. Thus, in calculating the rents presented in Table II.B.4, Indonesian cost estimates were used. Rents for logs were apparently higher than those for sawn timber in every year except 1980, peaking at a level 2.4 times higher in 1982. Thus, domestic processing at the expense of log exports dissipated economic rents for most of the period.

As Table II.B.5 shows, total rents dropped precipitously from US$635 million in 1979 to only US$305 million in 1983, though log and

Table II.B.4. Sabah: Aggregate Rents in Tropical Timber 1979–83

Year	(1) Potential Rent Per m³ of Logs US$ per m³ᵃ	(2) Volume of Log Exports millions of m³ (RWE)	(3) Total Log Rent US$ millions (1) × (2)	(4) Sawnmilling Potential Rent per m³ of Sawntimber in Roundwood Equivalent US$ per m³ᵃ
1979	64.12	9.72	623.2	63.25
1980	62.39	8.21	512.2	71.87
1981	46.34	8.69	402.70	26.93
1982	50.75	9.83	498.87	20.93
1983	30.39	9.48	288.10	17.75

Year	(5) Volume of Sawntimber Exports in million m³ (RWE)	(6) Total Rent in Milling (4) × (5) US$ million	(7) Total Rent in Logging and Milling (3) + (6) US$ million
1979	0.19	12.0	635.2
1980	0.29	20.8	533.0
1981	0.39	10.50	413.2
1982	0.64	13.39	512.3
1983	0.94	16.69	304.8

sawn timber export volumes grew slightly. This reflects falling f.o.b. export prices, and rising logging and milling costs. *(See Table II.B.4).*

Over the period 1979–1982 the government collected 83 percent of total rents, *(See Table II.B.5)* by combining forceful tax policies and royalties that were progressive with respect to world price increases.

Arguably, however, timber has been sold too quickly: the area of undisturbed forest decreased from 55 percent of the state's total land area in 1973 to only 25 percent by 1983. Timber production might decline dramatically by as early as 1990 as lands available for harvesting continue to diminish.

Sarawak

Sarawak is 68 percent larger than neighboring Sabah. Some 9.4 million of its 12.5 million hectares are in forests, one-third of which government fully controls.

In Sarawak, swamp forests cover 1.5 million hectares, 16 percent of the total forested area, and hill forests account for virtually all of the rest. Swamp forests have been exploited for decades. By now, most of the valuable stands of *ramin* have been cut, although a significant amount of commercially desirable *Shorea albida* remains. Logging shifted after 1970 toward harvesting the mixed *Dipterocarp* hill forests, and by 1978 more timber was being removed from

Table II.B.5. Sabah: Rent Capture by Government 1979–83

	Total Aggregate Rents in Forest-Based Activity (Logging plus milling) US$ millions[a]	Total Royalties and Taxes on Forest-Based Activity US$ millions[b]	Proportion of Rent Captured by Government (2) ÷ (1)
1979	635.2	511.6	80.5
1980	533.0	488.4	91.6
1981	413.2	342.1	82.8
1982	512.3	360.9	70.4
1983	304.8	283.8	93.1

them than from swamp forests. Even so, only about 41 percent of hill forests were under concession by 1980, while almost all swamp forests were.

Deforestation in Sarawak has accelerated over the last decade, though not as rapidly as in Sabah. *(See Table II.B.1.)* By 1985, about 89,000 hectares per year were deforested, nearly one percent of the total forest area. Shifting cultivation has accounted for perhaps 27,000 to 60,000 hectares per year, and may have affected as much as 3.7 million hectares by 1985, one-third of the state's forested land. Per capita income in Sarawak is only about half the national average, and some 230,000 people, 20 percent of population, survive through shifting cultivation.

Logging for direct export has been the other main cause, though its precise effect on the deforestation rate is unknown. In contrast to Sabah's, the wood products industry in Sarawak is still small, because the government has not instituted log export restrictions or taxes to stimulate growth in this sector.

Benefits from Timber Exploitation

The forest sector has contributed substantially to the state's gross regional product. From 1971 to 1984, annual timber export earnings increased rapidly, from US$70 million to nearly US$600 million. Forest sector employment growth nearly doubled between 1978 to 1984, by which time roughly 22,000 people—9 percent of Sarawak's labor force worked in forest-based activities. Forest charges accounted for 20 to 25 percent of total government revenues through most of the 1970s, before increasing to nearly 50 percent in 1982 as royalty charges increased. But revenues never accounted for more than 18.3 percent of gross export values, much less than in Sabah and even Indonesia, where comparable figures were 59 and 32.6 percent, respectively. Sarawak's low percentage return reflects the lower quality and accessibility of its hardwood stands, the early depletion of its valuable *ramin* stocks, and government policies that were not designed to capture available rents effectively.

Forestry Policies

With the exception of an *ad valorem* export tax, all timber fees are volume-based. Of these, the royalty, which is differentiated by species, is by far the most substantial. The export tax, applied only to logs, was only 5 percent until 1980, when it was doubled. Still, it provides only a limited incentive for domestic processing.

The various charges produce revenues only on the order of US$19.25 per cubic meter of *Dipterocarp* logs at 1980 f.o.b. prices of US$100 per cubic meter. If f.o.b. values rise to US$150 per cubic meter, the government's share increases only to US$24.25—29 percent of the revenue taken at the same f.o.b. prices in Sabah.

In Sarawak concessions are granted for a maximum of ten years, and many are assigned for only one or five years. The poorly defined and enforced harvesting system requires essentially no silvicultural management, and government forest programs have focussed almost exclusively on timber, ignoring such profitable or potentially profitable non-wood products as rattan, fruits, nuts, oils, and pharmaceutical goods. Certain products, especially wild game, have long been an economic mainstay for the state's indigenous people. Detailed studies reveal that as much as 35,500 tons of meat, worth US$82 million, have been taken annually.

On the other hand, lower royalties in Sarawak and the differentiated royalty structure that assigns much lower charges to less valuable species discourage high-grading. An estimated 58 percent of the remaining stems in Sarawak have no damage after logging, while only 26 percent are unaffected in Sabah. Also, the number of broken or missing trees in logged-over stands in Sarawak is only 14.6 percent, compared to nearly 62 percent in Sabah.

Peninsular Malaysia

Peninsular Malaysia's twelve states cover about 13.2 million hectares, an area roughly equal to that of Sarawak. Eighty-one percent of all Malaysians live on the peninsula, 48 percent of which is covered by forest.

Deforestation has been rapid and steady since 1900. Thirty percent of the natural forests were lost between 1910 and 1980, with 13 percent eliminated from 1950 to 1980 alone. By 1985, an estimated 90,000 hectares, or 1.4 percent of the remaining forested lands, were being cleared each year. (See Table II.B.1.) Conversion to permanent agriculture accounts for 90 percent of total deforestation over the last decade, though logging played a major role from 1955 until 1980. Shifting cultivation has

been insignificant in West Malaysian deforestation.

Benefits from Timber Exploitation

In the mid-1970s, the forest-based sector produced 2 to 3 percent of the region's gross domestic product. Wood export earnings tripled between 1971 and 1978, when they accounted for 7 percent of total peninsular exports. The sector also provided 43,000 jobs in 1978 and more than 67,000 in 1984 (0.1 percent of the total labor force).

Benefits from converting forests to agriculture have been large. Steady agricultural growth made West Malaysia the world's leading exporter of rubber and palm oil by 1970, supporting the growth of per capita income to US$1860 by 1983, a level three times higher than in Indonesia, and helping to reduce rural poverty.

Government Policies

No unified discussion of forestry policies in West Malaysia is possible because each of the twelve states jealously guards its autonomy in land and forest management. Each state collects timber revenues, grants concessions, and restricts harvesting methods. Attempts to integrate policies have met with limited success. A Uniform National Forestry Policy that limited the extent and techniques of harvesting allowed was approved by the National Land Council in 1978, but states control implementation and enforcement.

Regional industrial development plans have been more widely accepted. Mainly log-export quotas have been used to implement this policy. Begun in 1972, restrictions were progressively tightened so that virtually no logs were exported after 1978. This approach brought nearly 600 sawmills and 40 plywood/veneer mills into operation by 1984. However, low recovery rates in the region's mills relative to those in Europe and Japan mean that more timber must be harvested for a given output of product than under more efficient systems, and the strong industrial constituency may force policy-makers to keep output levels high even when global demand is low.

The Philippines

From the late 1950s through 1973, deforestation in the Philippines reached 172,000 hectares per year. Virgin forests have been especially hard hit, declining by 1.7 million hectares from 1971 to 1980 alone. In 1982, fifty-five percent of the Philippines' total land area (16.6 million hectares) was classified as forested land and virgin forests accounted for about 9 percent (2.7 million hectares). However, 1976 Landsat photos showed only 8.5 to 9.0 million hectares actually under forests, and 1983 photos revealed a decrease to 7.8 to 8.3 million hectares, within which virgin forests were only 2.0 to 2.5 million hectares.

An important source of deforestation has been the dramatic expansion of destructive logging. After independence, the Philippines' new government viewed exploitation of the country's forest reserves as a good way to raise desperately needed revenues. Log- and wood-product exports were resumed, and timber companies were given substantial incentives. (Porter 1987.) Harvests quickly increased to more than 5 million cubic meters in the late 1950s. Driven by incentives, strength in the world log market, and mechanized harvesting, the timber boom continued during the 1960s, peaking in 1969. By then, the annual harvest exceeded 11 million cubic meters, nearly triple that of 1955. As the timber boom gained momentum, the government was unable to supervise concessions effectively or enforce logging regulations. Links between timber companies and politicians further eroded government control. Annual outputs averaging 10 million cubic meters were maintained until 1974, when depletion, world recession, and competition from other log-exporting countries forced a reduction. Declines continued over the next decade, and by 1984 the harvest had

After independence, the Philippines' new government viewed exploitation of the country's forest reserves as a good way to raise desperately needed revenues, but as the timber boom gained momentum, the government was unable to supervise concessions effectively or enforce logging regulations.

returned to the pre-boom level of 3.8 million cubic meters.

Shifting cultivation has also helped degrade Philippine forests. Some 80,000 to 120,000 families cleared an estimated 2.3 million hectares of forest land. As elsewhere, the spread of shifting cultivation largely reflects population growth and the economy's failure to provide employment alternatives for the country's rural poor. Furthermore, deforestation has devastated the hill communities that relied on the forests for fruit, game, and other non-wood products for much of their livelihood.

Deforestation has left upper watersheds unprotected, destabilizing river flows, with significant effects on fish populations and agriculture. Soil erosion and sediment flows have increased dramatically. The implications for hydroelectric projects and irrigation facilities have already become apparent in Luzon, where anticipated lifetimes of the three most important reservoirs have been cut in half by sedimentation.

The often illegal conversion of mangrove forests to fishponds has also contributed to forest decline. Already, about 100,000 hectares, an area equivalent to roughly half of all Philippine mangrove forests remaining in 1982, has been lost.

History of Forest Policies

Four distinct periods characterize Philippine forest history. The first was one of low-level exploitation during colonial, wartime, and pre-independence eras. Forest degradation was negligible around 1900, when the United States gained control of the islands. Timber harvesting gradually increased until by the outbreak of World War II the logging industry was among the leading employers.

Exploitation and forest damage grew during the second period, after independence in 1946, when ownership of all forest lands was nationalized. As industry became more mechanized, large-scale logging expanded to meet strong postwar U.S. demand. Forest products, only 1.5 percent of total exports as late as 1949, grew to 11 percent by 1955.

Starting in 1961, a surge in Japanese demand triggered a dramatic increase in harvesting. Over the next fifteen years, harvests averaged 8.8 million cubic meters, more than twice pre-boom levels. Forest area under logging concessions nearly doubled, from 5.5 million hectares in 1960 to 10.6 million hectares in 1971, and forest products became the leading export commodity, reaching 33 percent of gross export values by 1969. The increased foreign exchange earnings and revenues pleased government officials, but lenient state policies and lax administration gave them little control over the multi-national and wealthy local concession holders who reaped huge profits at the expense of the forest estate and the government treasury.

During the timber boom, log output accounted for up to 80 percent of annual production value. In the decade since the boom slowed—a third period—government policy shifted to developing a strong wood-processing industry. The first attempts began in the late 1960s, when concessions went preferentially to companies that agreed to establish lumber and plywood mills. In 1967, a government directive required all harvesters to build processing plants and progressively reduce log exports. Many companies complied by building small, inefficient, and little-used mills, while continuing to export logs. As a result, in 1977 sawmills and plymills were operating at only 29 and 35 percent of capacity, respectively. The Marcos administration responded in 1975 with a ban on log exports and other policies to develop the industry. Pressure from logging interests kept government from implementing the ban fully, but partial bans and log export ceilings have been established. Reported log export volume declined to only 11 percent of total production by 1980. However, log exporting remains lucrative, and many firms underreport their actual log exports.

In the fourth period of Philippine forestry, conservation efforts have increased in the face of obvious forest depletion and damage from decades of unchecked exploitation. The log export ban, in addition to promoting processing industries, was a controversial attempt to reintroduce the sustained-yield management that had been lost in the timber boom. Unfortunately, deferral and weakening of log export restrictions along with increased log smuggling have reduced this policy's impact on forest destruction. Even less effective have been reductions in concessionaires' annual allowable cuts. Harvests have long been much less than AAC because of flaws in the formula used to determine it.

Several federal programs, including reforestation, industrial tree plantations, and social forestry, have been adopted to regenerate forest resources. Although the replanting effort has been expanded to include citizen, industry, and government participation, only an estimated 78,000 hectares had been reforested by 1983. Overall program performance has been poor for many reasons: funding has been inadequate, corruption is common, many projects are relegated to poor sites with marginal soils and steep slopes, and perhaps only 50 percent of all firms comply with industrial reforestation regulations.

The Integrated Social Forestry Program was recently established to solve the problem of shifting cultivation. Families in selected areas are given tenure to land they have occupied for 25 years, so that they will adopt sustainable farming systems. In 1983, the government supplied over 12 million seedlings to launch this program. Unfortunately, the program's effectiveness has also been limited by financial, managerial, and ecological constraints.

Forest Sector Policies

The timber boom was driven by the vast profits that logging companies accumulated because the government was unable to capture an appropriate share of resource rents through forest revenue systems. Forest taxes and fees amounted to only 0.5 to 1.3 percent of total government revenues over the 1970s.

For many years, the primary revenue source was a volume-based charge that ranged from 0.6 to 3.5 pesos per cubic meter, depending on timber quality. The rates, which were not adjusted for inflation, amounted to an insignificant fraction of the profits on the sale of mature timber. Other volume-based charges have been imposed to finance reforestation, extension, research and development, and other programs. Total volume-based charges amounted to 6.35 to 9.35 pesos per cubic meter for logs used domestically, and 10.85 to 13.25 pesos per cubic meter for exported logs. These fees were consolidated in 1980 to a charge of 20 pesos per cubic meter, and raised by 50 percent to US$1.52 in 1984. Secondary charges levied on timber harvesters include an annual license fee and one-time license application fee on concessions; a municipal graduated sales tax; and a realty tax of one percent of the assessed value of concession lands. Furthermore, since 1970, a manufacturer's sales tax has been collected at the rate of 10 percent of the gross value of domestic wood and wood products sales. The export tax is assessed at 20 percent of f.o.b. value for logs, 4 percent for lumber, and 14 percent for veneer. A 4 percent tax on plywood exports was eliminated in 1984.

As Table II.C.1. shows, revenues averaged only 8.8 percent of the sector's export values from 1970 through 1982—an indication of the government's failure to capture rents. During the timber boom peak in the late 1960s, the government collected an even smaller fraction of available rents: volume-base charges were lower, and neither sales nor realty taxes were imposed. (See Table II.C.2.) Between 1979 and 1982 the potential rents for sawn wood and logs were as much as 7.5 times greater than those for plywood on a roundwood equivalent basis. (See Table II.C.2). Indeed, in 1981 and 1982 there were economic losses on plywood production, partly because of inefficiencies in heavily protected plymills.

Government revenues in the Philippines averaged only 8.8 percent of the sector's export values from 1970 through 1982.

From 1979 to 1982, potential rents on the total log harvest totaled more than US$1.5 billion. (See Table II.C.3.) Over the same four years, the forest sector actually generated rents of slightly more than US$1 billion. The US$500 million loss in potential rents occurred because an increasing volume of logs was processed in inefficient domestic plymills rather than exported as logs or lumber.

From 1979 to 1982, government forest revenues totaled only US$171 million. As Table II.C.4. indicates, it captured only 12 percent of the US$1 billion in available rents. The remaining 88 percent, more than US$820 million, remained with private timbering interests and their allies as abnormal profits. As a percentage of potential timber rents, public revenues were even less, averaging 11 percent. These tremendous incentives explain the industry's rapid

Table II.C.1. Taxes as Percentage of Reported Export Values of Logs, Lumber, Plywood and Veneer for 1970–82

Year	Total Taxes from Forest Sector (million pesos)	Total Reported Exports (million pesos)	Taxes as % of Exports
1970	207	1666	12.4
1971	235	1623	14.5
1972	124	1455	8.5
1973	228	2788	8.2
1974	135	1859	7.3
1975	111	1682	6.6
1976	127	2006	6.3
1977	125	1975	6.3
1978	134	2404	5.6
1979	419	3757	11.2
1980	294	3405	8.6
1981	338	2715	12.4
1982	367	2479	14.8

Table II.C.2. Potential Rent of Logs, Lumber and Plywood in Roundwood Equivalent (RWE) in US$

Year	Product	Average Value Per m³ Product	RWE	Per m³ Production Cost	RWE	Potential Rent Per m³ (RWE)
	Logs	116	116	47	47	69
1979	Lumber	217	131		56	75
	Plywood	263	113		103	10
	Logs	127	127	49	49	78
1980	Lumber	242	145		61	84
	Plywood	326	141		114	27
	Logs	106	106	51	51	55
1981	Lumber	230	138		63	75
	Plywood	280	120		123	−3
	Logs	111	111	54	54	57
1982	Lumber	209	125		67	58
	Plywood	280	120		131	−11
	Logs	93	93	59	59	34
1983	Lumber	204	123		74	49
	Plywood	260	112		146	−34

Table II.C.3. Aggregate Rents in Timber: Logs, Lumber and Plywood for 1979–82

Year	Total Log Harvest ('000 m³)	Rent per m³ US$	Potential Rent ('000 US$)
1979	6578	69	453882
1980	6352	78	495456
1981	4514	55	248270
1982	5400	57	307800

LOGS

Year	Net Production ('000 m³)	Rent per m³ (US$)	Aggregate Rent ('000 US$)
1979	1496	69	103224
1980	1265	78	98670
1981	360	55	19800
1982	1680	57	95760

LUMBER

Year	Production in RWE* ('000 m³)	Rent per m³ (US$)	Aggregate Rent ('000 US$)
1979	2699	75	202425
1980	2538	84	213192
1981	2023	75	151725
1982	1992	58	115536

PLYWOOD

Year	Production in RWE* ('000 m³)	Rent per m³ (US$)	Aggregate Rent ('000 US$)
1979	1166	10	11660
1980	1282	27	34614
1981	1060	-3	-3180
1982	979	-11	-10769

TOTAL ACTUAL RENT

Year	('000 US$)
1979	317309
1980	346476
1981	168345
1982	200527

expansion, surreptitious log exports, and evasion of logging restrictions. *(See Table II.C.4.)*

Concessions of from one to ten years granted through the 1970s provided concessionaires with few incentives to practice sustained-yield management. Concessions have since been extended to 25 years, with potential for renewal for an additional 25 years, but these are still short relative to the 70-year growing cycles of many tropical species. Harvesters thus still concentrate on maximizing their return through immediate exploitation of the resource.

The effects of excessive rents and short-term leases have been compounded by the structure of forest charges. For instance, failing to adequately differentiate forest charges by timber grade, species, and accessibility and basing charges on the volume cut rather than on the volume of merchantable timber available may have encouraged high-grading, the logging of larger areas to produce the same output, and carelessness toward unharvested trees.

Weak enforcement of regulations on harvesting methods, stand improvement, and forest protection has also contributed to the problem. Funding and personnel to supervise private loggers have been chronically short since the timber boom began, so harvesters can easily avoid the restrictions that minimize logging damage.

Forest-Based Industrialization

The Philippine government's program to develop the wood-processing industry had four main goals: to increase foreign exchange, to create domestic value-added, to stimulate employment, and to use dwindling forest resources more effectively. Processed wood exports, mainly lumber and plywood, increased as a share of total sectoral exports from 14 percent in 1970 to 76 percent in 1983. The value of processed wood exports peaked in 1979 at US$317 million, but by 1983 had declined by 20 percent amid the world recession. The number of processing plants also declined: from a peak in 1976, the number of operating sawmills fell from 325 to 190 in 1982, plymills from 209 to only 35, and veneer mills from 23 to 11.

These reductions occurred despite the industry's heavy effective protection, the result mostly of log export taxes and bans that depressed domestic log prices. These measures reduced the nominal rate of protection to logging from minus 6 percent in 1970 to 1975 to minus 46 percent by 1979 to 1980. (Bautista and Power 1979.) However, pulp and paper processing and other forest-based industries benefitted greatly: by the late 1970s, they had received some of the highest effective rates of protection among Philippine industries. Pulp-mills have also been exempted from certain harvesting restrictions and allowed to clearcut

Table II.C.4. Government Capture of Actual and Potential Timber Rents: 1979–82

	Potential Rent Without Processing (US$ million)	Actual Rent on Logs, Lumber & Plywood (US$ million)	Total Gov't Forest Revenues (US$ million)	Gov't Revenues as % of Potential Rents	Gov't Revenues as % of Actual Rents
1979	453.9	317.3	51.6	11	16
1980	495.5	346.5	33.6	7	10
1981	248.3	168.3	42.6	17	25
1982	307.8	200.5	42.9	14	21
	1505.5	1032.6	170.7	12	18

thousands of hectares of logged-over *Dipterocarp* forests for feedstock.

Inefficient plywood manufacturing also leads to deforestation. Plywood is produced at a rate of 2.32 cubic meters of logs per cubic meter of output, a conversion factor of only 43 percent, compared to up to 58 percent elsewhere in Asia. Philippine sawmills are somewhat more efficient, requiring 1.66 cubic meters of logs per cubic meter of lumber, a conversion factor of 60 percent.

Inefficiencies in the industry also reduce potential rents as higher costs absorb profits. For instance, in 1983 a cubic meter of plywood in roundwood equivalent that was worth US$112 cost US$146 to produce, implying a rent of minus US$34 per cubic meter. In addition the government lost US$18 per cubic meter of log used for plywood—money that would have been captured from export taxes on unprocessed logs.

Greater processing efficiency made sawmills much more valuable to the country. Resource rents from lumber exports surpassed those for unprocessed logs from 1979 through 1983, averaging US$68 per cubic meter of roundwood equivalent as compared to US$58 per cubic meter of raw logs. The Philippines should ultimately have a comparative advantage in both timber production and processing, if sustained-yield management can be instituted. On the other hand, if destructive logging is continued, the associated ecological costs must be evaluated, and may drastically reduce the net returns in the forest sector.

Conversion of Forests to Other Uses

Since the early 1900s, government policies that have distributed public forest lands to the landless and poor have accelerated deforestation. Through the 1960s, the government encouraged settlements in virgin forest to broaden the economy's agricultural base. When the population remained relatively small, no dramatic damages ensued, but as population growth increased after World War II, pressures on forest reserves became increasingly severe.

The single most important such program has been the ''land for the landless'' program established in the 1950s and 1960s. From 1959 to 1963, this policy alone caused the conversion of 100,000 hectares of forested land per year for farming. (Puyat 1972.) The Manahan Act and the Homestead Act, which also allowed the conversion of occupied forests to agriculture, combined to convert as much as 200,000 hectares per year over those decades.

From 1959 to 1963, the Philippines' ''land for the landless'' program caused the conversion of 100,000 hectares of forested land per year for farming.

Shifting cultivation has also helped degrade both lowland and upland forests. Many uplanders traditionally relied on swidden agriculture, alternating cropping with fallow in a sustainable cycle. However, population growth has forced a shortening of fallow periods, lowering soil fertility. Furthermore, with deepening poverty, lowlanders now rely primarily on shifting cultivation for survival. As logging and related road development accelerate, new areas became accessible, affecting thousands of hectares of forest.

In 1975, the government finally responded to the situation by allowing farmers to occupy 5 hectares of the land they tilled for up to 50 years. Sustainable management practices outlining the planting of certain trees and crops were prescribed. However, inferior terrain, continuous cultivation, and poor farming and soil conservation techniques have quickly reduced productivity and increased erosion in many of these projects.

China

China is acutely short of forest resources. Although ranking sixth in the world in total area, the forest area amounts only to 0.12 hectares per capita, 18 percent of the world average. *(See Table II.D.1)*

Wood scarcity has forced Chinese industry to use substitutes that reduce product quality. Some 9 million cubic meters of wood are imported annually, and rural households have suffered acute fuel shortages. (National Conference on Wood 1983.) Depletion of forest resources has aggravated soil erosion, desertification, and stream sedimentation. Soil loss totals about 5 billion tons a year, with a nutrient value equal to 40 million tons of chemical fertilizer, double the quantity farmers actually use. Devegetation of slopes by fuel-hungry peasants is an important source of erosion. (Dowdle 1987.)

Government policy in the People's Republic has been critical since forests have been state-owned and forest product industries subject to central planning. In the planned sector, wood prices have been kept artificially low, without adequate differentials for species, quality, or dimension. Low prices weakened incentives for consumers to use wood efficiently and led producers to ignore consumer needs.

Although central planning met high-priority allocations, it only covered one quarter of total timber output. Off-plan production, which met local and noncommercial needs, was marketed more flexibly. Still, constraints on such trade impaired efficiency, especially during the Cultural Revolution, when producers and traders were subject to severe sanctions.

State investment failed to compensate for low commodity prices. Profit remissions and tax payments by state forest enterprises to the treasury exceeded public investments. Investment priorities were also skewed. For example, the wood panels industry, which might have raised conversion efficiency, was badly neglected. Management and technological shortcomings also contributed to an enormous waste of usable wood fiber. Only about 37 percent of harvested fiber was made into commodities. Large quantities of wood were left in the forests, discarded in timber yards, or diverted to lower priority uses.

China is acutely short of forest resources. Although ranking sixth in the world in total area, China's forest area amounts only to 0.12 hectares per capita, 18 percent of the world average.

To remedy the forest deficit, the government instituted massive afforestation campaigns after 1949. Plantings averaged 4 to 5 million hectares a year. Although the programs met with striking success in some areas, the overall situation remained serious.

Following the change of leadership after Chairman Mao Zedong's death in the late 1970s, China tried to speed economic development by increasing economic efficiency and the use of intellectual capital. Chinese socialism still involved state ownership of land and a continuing state role in production and distribution, but it was clear that significant changes were needed in price policy, marketing, and management.

Pre-Reform Pricing Policy

Prior to reforms, administered prices were so low that growers had no incentive or funds to reinvest in forestry, and sometimes they absorbed losses, while consumers persistently wasted wood. As Table II.D.2 shows, retail prices remained constant from 1955 until 1972 and did not rise appreciably until 1979. Price differentials for species, quality, and size were

Table II.D.1. Provincial Forestry Resources 1981

Province	Forested Land		Volume of Standing Timber on Forested Land	
	Thousand Hectares	% of Land Area	Thousand Cubic Meters	% of National Total
Beijing	143.8	8.1	1,465.9	0.02
Tianjin	29.9	2.6	187.0	0.00
Hebei	1,676.8	9.0	26,495.1	0.29
Shanxi	810.0	5.2	33,339.9	0.37
Inner Mongolia	13,740.1	1.9	847,776.3	9.39
Liaoning	3,652.7	25.1	100,393.5	1.11
Jilin	6,078.9	32.2	656,974.5	7.28
Heilongjiang	15,294.4	33.6	1,436,628.4	15.91
Shanghai	7.9	1.3	18.8	0.00
Jiangsu	324.7	3.2	3,226.4	0.04
Zhejiang	3,428.9	33.7	79,183.3	0.88
Anhui	1,791.6	13.0	54,583.5	0.61
Fujian	4,496.4	37.0	296,379.8	3.28
Jiangxi	5,462.3	32.8	236,328.0	2.62
Shandong	904.7	5.9	4,837.4	0.05
Henan	1,419.9	8.5	31,885.1	0.35
Hubei	3,779.0	20.3	98,604.1	1.09
Hunan	6,872.3	32.5	160,210.2	1.77
Guangdong	5,878.6	27.7	203,406.1	2.25
Guangxi	5,227.2	22.7	220,661.8	2.45
Sichuan	6,810.8	12.0	1,048,804.2	11.62
Guizhou	2,309.3	13.1	126,405.0	1.40
Yunnan	9,196.5	24.0	1,097,033.0	12.15
Tibet	6,320.3	5.1	1,400,524.6	15.51
Shaanxi	4,471.4	12.7	251,532.7	2.79
Gansu	1,769.0	3.9	164,020.5	1.82
Qinghai	194.5	0.3	17,154.2	0.19
Ningxia	95.1	1.4	2,769.7	0.03
Xinjiang	1,120.9	0.7	200,278.3	2.22
Taiwan	1,969.5	55.1	226,846.0	2.51
TOTAL	115,277.4	12.0	9,027,953.3	100.00

Source: Dangdai Zhonggo de Linye [Contemporary China's Forestry] 1985.

Table II.D.2. Procurement and Retail Prices for Timber and Timber Products 1952–84[a]

Year	Timber Procurement Prices (yuan/cubic meter)	Average Timber Retail Prices (yuan/cubic meter)
1952–56 (average)	20	91
1957–61 (average)	22	100
1962–66 (average)	35	100
1967–71 (average)	37	100
1972–76 (average)	39	106
1977	37	108
1978	37	109
1979	43	120
1980	56	149
1981	62	197
1982	72	216
1983	78	215
1984	—	265

Notes:

a. Prices are nominal or current year prices. Procurement prices are average prices across all species and grades and represent a mix of posted procurement prices, negotiated prices, and above-quota prices, at least since 1978. Retail prices are average prices for all species and grades of timber.

Source: State Statistical Bureau; *State Statistical Yearbook* 1985: 537.

also overly narrow, encouraging consumers to requisition superior timber in unnecessarily large quantities. Growers had little reason to raise more valuable species and processors had no incentive to mill efficiently.

Although prices of all agricultural products and other primary commodities were depressed relative to prices for finished goods in China, the effect on forests was relatively more severe. Administered prices were calculated on the basis of allowable costs plus taxes and a profit margin, but without capital charges, even though forests take years to mature and also suffer significant damage before harvest. Omitting capital charges thus harmed forestry more than industries with annual production cycles.

In addition, production cost calculations were skewed against forest management because the costs of growing timber, as contrasted with harvesting and processing it, were long ignored under the assumption that trees were gifts of nature. Only on timber plantations were growing costs reimbursable (at unusually low rates based on pre-1949 reference prices). At most, prices barely covered direct operating costs, providing a virtually zero return to producers.

The silvicultural fee served as a surrogate for stumpage prices, but only covered costs incurred in the first three years after planting, which discouraged thinning and other operations after the three-year limit. Nor were fees

Prior to reforms, administered prices for forest products in China were so low that growers had no incentive or funds to reinvest in forestry, and sometimes they absorbed losses, while consumers persistently wasted wood.

necessarily returned to the original production areas; some were allocated to other jurisdictions in need of afforestation or diverted to other purposes. Ironically, the silvicultural fee encouraged enterprises to log the most accessible and lowest quality timber first, and shortened the optimum rotation, because it reduced the relative price premium for larger, higher-quality trees.

Some allowance was made for grower costs in collective forests, but very low government procurement prices enforced through compulsory deliveries were held virtually constant for the decade starting in the mid-1950s, after which authorized increases were still only modest.

Market and Management Problems

State planning and distribution systems created problems matching supplies to demands. All logs had to be shipped through Forestry Ministry timber yards for sorting. This extra step inflated handling costs, caused delays, and reduced log quality due to poor storage. Anticipating delays, handlers and end users expanded inventories to insulate themselves against supply interruptions, lowering efficiency in the entire system. Producers tended to process and deliver timber according to the incentives signalled by irrational prices. The supply of items with attractive posted prices, such as transmission poles, exceeded demand five fold. Supplies of such items as railroad

ties, for which posted prices tended to be low, suffered 50 percent shortfalls below production quotas. (Kaixin 1983.)

Perhaps fortunately, the limited coverage of the state plan restricted state control. Off-plan production of non commercial fuelwood and below-grade timber created alternative supply sources, but distorted planners' perspective. State forest farms used their own timber profligately since they benefitted little from additional deliveries to the state distribution system. They also produced below-grade timber that could be bartered with other enterprises.

Management presented additional issues. Most of China's forests are administered by the Ministry of Forestry, but actual management is primarily provincial and local. State forest farms are grouped into a smaller number of forestry bureaus in the forest districts. Although forest management and forest industry are formally joined at the ministry level and often at lower levels, the two branches operate independently for many purposes, and divisions and rivalry recur. Industry is responsible for logging and local processing, and it gets most state investment. Management is responsible for afforestation, regeneration, and cultivation. The separation of duties leads the industry to disregard forest replacement costs (e.g., by adopting logging procedures and slash disposal practices that hamper regeneration).

Since forest farms are located in remote areas, they must assume some of the functions of local governments and provide employment, hospitals, schools and other services—all based on a dwindling resource base. As forests are depleted, the bureaus must continue to work the stands and improvise to provide employment for a permanent, immobile labor force and finance services for their growing population.

Similar problems hampered the collective sector. The recession after the Great Leap Forward (1959 to 1961) resulted in a partial devolution of authority back to production team and intermediate-level production brigades within the communes, but the locus of authority remained unstable and uncertain, with dire consequences for forestry. Although production teams were the units of acccount, most collectively owned forests were operated by larger production brigades reluctant to relinquish control. Centralization bred continuing resentment among neighboring collectives over encroachment on their property, which in turn encouraged poaching and preemptive liquidation on standing forests to prevent others from capturing valuable assets. Production teams were also reluctant to send their best workers to the collective forest farms because any profits from them accrued to their parent units.

Countermeasures

In the late 1970s, analysts realized that a new pricing system was needed so that silviculture would become profitable and self-sustaining. Because prices had been so low for so long, overall price increases were needed to incorporate fully all costs including interest charges. Finer price distinctions among species, grades and sizes of wood products were also needed. Corollary changes were also needed in marketing policy to make distribution more efficient.

Recalculating Administrative Prices

The critical first step in adjusting the administrative price structure was to account in product prices for all growing and management costs. The costs of growing trees are inversely related to soil and land climatic conditions: the better the land and the more favorable the climatic conditions the lower the costs. Predicating the pricing system on the growing costs on average or superior land, however, would discourage forest cultivation on inferior land and deprive producers on superior land of economic rents. Calculating stumpage prices in accordance with growing costs on inferior land would provide incentives for low cost pro-

ducers to engage in forestry. Taxes could still reduce economic rents enjoyed by those on superior land so as to control income disparities.

The new administrative prices consisted primarily of production costs on inferior land. But capital charges representing the value of time were incorporated in the price formula to account for the opportunity costs of capital while timber remained on the stump. In the past, when the banking and credit systems were peripheral to investment finance, such charges had been disregarded and depreciation allowances were also unrealistically low. Insurance costs against losses due to fire, pests, disease, wind throws, and floods, for which the

---

Capital charges representing the value of time were incorporated in the price formula to account for the opportunity costs of capital while timber remained on the stump.

---

grower was not reimbursed, were also incorporated into prices. First investigated in 1982, pilot insurance projects began in 1984. Today more than 10 provinces have forest insurance systems. In addition, a profit margin is now included for reinvestment and incentive purposes. Currently, profit is calculated not only on the industry side (which includes logging, transportation, and milling, as was historically the case), but is also a component of management costs. Lastly, administrative prices provide for tax payments, as China's fiscal system shifts from reliance on profit remission by state-owned enterprises toward tax revenues.

The new method of price calculation recognizes that costs per unit of standing timber are highest in the first few years after planting and fall as trees mature. Stumpage prices reflect accumulated costs, including capital charges, on an annualized basis. *(See Table II.D.3.)*

Table II.D.3. Average and Marginal Production Costs Including Interest Charges for a Hypothetical Masson's Pine Plantation[a]

Age of Stand (years)	Aggregate Costs (yuan/ha)	Timber Yield m³	Marginal Costs (yuan/ha)	Average Cost (yuan/ha)[b]
8	1,519.5	13.7	43.8	110.9
12	2,301.0	35.7	24.3	64.5
16	3,154.5	58.8	24.9	53.6
20	4,282.5	95.6	37.1	44.8
24	5,770.5	127.1	65.2	45.4
28	8,022.0	155.4	76.5	51.6
32	11,047.5	170.1	89.5	64.9
36	14,701.5	216.3	120.4	68.0
40	19,525.5	247.8	158.9	78.8

Notes:
a. Costs include interest charges.
b. Average cost = Aggregate costs (including interest charges)/total timber reserves.

This pricing system also indicates the optimum rotation age, which occurs when average costs are at a minimum. As Figure II.D.3 shows, optimum rotation periods can vary from 20 to 25 years for poplar to over 60 years for Korean pine.

Administered prices increasingly function as floor prices as market distribution mechanisms develop and consumers express their demand in monetary terms. Wider administrative price differentials are being instituted to foster conservation and discourage demand for relatively high-cost products.

Implementation of Price Reforms

Price increases were implemented in several stages in order to reduce inflationary shocks and also because equilibrium levels were unclear when the entire commodity price structure was being revised. In the southern collective forest districts, log-procurement prices and timber-yard gate prices rose by an average of 30.6 percent and 20.3 percent, respectively, in

1979, and by an additional 36 and 20 percent, respectively, in 1981. No further price increases took place during the next five years because the government budget could not support higher timber procurement prices and transfer payment to consumers to cover their higher costs.

In the state forestry sector, producer prices rose by an average of 30 percent in 1980, 10 percent in 1981 and again in 1983, and by a further 44 percent in 1986, when previous increases proved insufficient. The price increases widened the differentials between the superior species and ordinary hardwoods from 1:1.57 to 1:2.25 and reduced the differential between sawnwood and logs from 1:2.5 to 1:1.7 to give the grower a larger share of the revenues.

Market and Management Reform

Beginning in the late 1970s controls over the collective forest districts were relaxed, first by opening timber markets (in which consumers

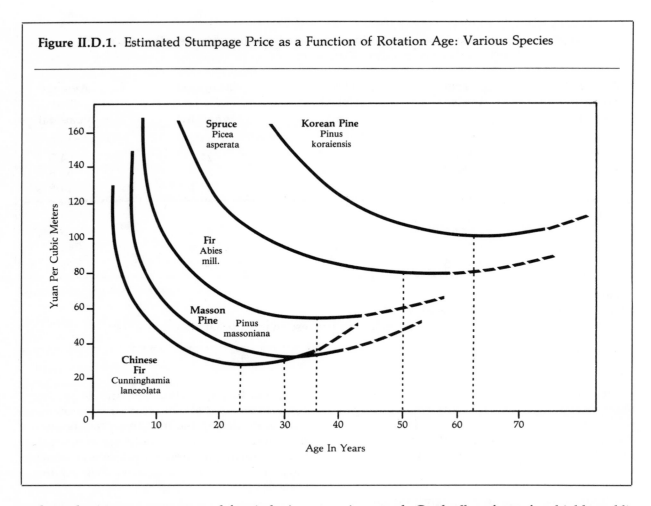

Figure II.D.1. Estimated Stumpage Price as a Function of Rotation Age: Various Species

Spruce
Picea
asperata

Korean Pine
Pinus
koraiensis

Fir
Abies
mill.

Masson
Pine
Pinus
massoniana

Chinese
Fir
Cunninghamia
lanceolata

Yuan Per Cubic Meters

Age In Years

and purchasing agents competed for timber) throughout the districts. These markets partially displaced the old state monopoly system for purchase and distribution. The increase in market prices coincided with increased deforestation in parts of the country, which many foresters and conservative officials attributed to increased logging in response to market liberalization. Consumers who had to pay sharply higher prices for their timber and who found regular supply sources interrupted also complained.

In response, timber markets were closed in forest districts in 1980 and the size of the policy, procurement, and judiciary forces devoted to forestry affairs was markedly increased. Gradually, after a few highly publicized cases in which violators were punished, markets reopened. (Renwei 1986.) In 1985, the compulsory procurement system was officially abolished. This change did not eliminate price controls, but rather established a three-tier system in which a small fraction of output remained subject to compulsory state procurement (at the prices introduced in 1981), a second fraction was subject to purchase by the state at higher, above-quota prices, and a third was available for market sale. Even the market sales were regulated, however: both buyers and sellers were registered, price bands were set to limit upward price fluctuations, and forestry officials were authorized to limit the volume of sales to ensure that the local harvest did not exceed annual growth. State forestry units were allowed to market their produce, but to a lesser extent than collectives: state forest bureaus were allowed to sell a portion of their output at premium prices once they had satisfied their quotas.

Although at first prices rose sharply, by 1986 they were already stabilizing due to market adjustments, regulation, and the availability of imported wood to buffer excess demand. In general, the markets provided welcome flexibility and also enabled the authorities to supervise prices and transactions more closely. (State Statistical Yearbook 1983.)

With higher prices and wider differentials between timber of different quality, consumers seem to be increasingly quality conscious. Small-size miscellaneous wood and inferior timber have trouble finding buyers, while large and medium-sized logs are easy to sell. Superior quality timber remains in high demand while inferior timber remains unsold.

With higher prices and wider differentials between timber of different quality, Chinese consumers seem to be increasingly quality conscious.

Management institutions have changed dramatically along with distribution changes. The number of collective forest farms has declined so much that by 1984 the number of workers employed had been reduced by nearly 40 percent. To fill the gap, households and other small private entities have assumed a larger share of the work load. Fifty million households now manage 30 million hectares of private hills and 40 million hectares of forest land under a contract responsibility system that in its most common form resembles sharecropping. The collective retains ownership of the land but contracts with households or workers to manage the land for 15 to 20 years, or for the expected life of the stand, on a contract that may be inherited. Contractors receive income from the forests or woodlots, as well as rights to other income and commodities produced on the land. The 30 million hectares of private hills are supposed to be assigned to households on a permanent basis, and households need not pay a share of that income back to the collective. By 1985, households were conducting over 50 percent of an expanding afforestation effort around the country. Households also assumed responsibility for soil conservation measures on erodable land with the aid of state subsidies.

An essential ingredient in the expanded role of both household management and market-oriented forestry was the demarcation and enforcement of property rights. The authorities have defined more carefully and enforced both ownership and usage rights in forestry. The rights are inheritable and to a limited extent are alienable, it now being possible to sell immature timber.

Change within the larger state sector has been less extensive, but some effort has been made to transfer the management of specific tasks or sites to workers or dependents in groups or as individuals. Consumer localities and enterprises have been encouraged to invest in forestry operations elsewhere in the country. They enjoy an assured source of wood supply and simultaneously help to alleviate the critical capital shortage that has hampered forestry development.

Brazil

The Amazon region encompasses 5.5 million square kilometers, by far the world's largest tropical moist forest. Of this, roughly 3.8 million square kilometers lie within Brazil. The Brazilian forests are home to as many as one fifth of the world's plant and animal species

Fifty million households now manage 30 million hectares of private hills and 40 million hectares of forest land under a contract responsibility system that in its most common form resembles sharecropping.

and contain nearly one third of the world's broad-leafed timber, an estimated 48 to 78 million cubic meters with a market value of as much as US$1.7 trillion (at 1984 prices). (Knowles 1966; Browder 1986: 232.)

Despite these forest resources, Brazil's wood industry has not yet played a major role in the national economy. Timber products increased from only 6.1 percent of national industrial output in 1960 to 12.9 percent in 1980, but still accounted for only 4.9 percent of foreign exchange earnings. Brazil has been producing less than 10 percent of the world's supply of tropical wood products, but this share is expected to increase as reserves dwindle in Southeast Asia. (UNIDO 1983: 35.)

Within the Amazon region, however, the forest sector has been of vital economic importance. Wood products account for more than a quarter of industrial output in four of the region's six states, exceeding 60 percent in Rondônia and Roraima. The industry has expanded rapidly over the last twenty years, with the number of sawmills rising from 194 in 1965 to 1639 by 1981 and average output per mill more than doubling. The Amazon's share in national roundwood production doubled between 1975 and 1980.

Although deforestation in the Brazilian Amazon has caused considerable concern in recent years, the rate remains uncertain. The most widely accepted figures, government estimates based on Landsat data, indicate that roughly

14.8 million hectares of forest had been altered by 1983, approximately 3 percent of the area of the Legal Amazon region, (the states of Para, Amazonas, Acre, Rondônia, Amapá, Mato Grosso, and much of Goías and Maranhão). However, many scientists claim that the altered area may now be two to five times that large. (Fearnside 1985.) At any rate, the area deforested increased exponentially in several states in the 1970s. *(See Figure II.E.1.)*

Cattle ranching has been the foremost cause of forest conversion. Given an estimated herd of almost 9 million head in 1980 and an average stocking rate of one head per hectare, nearly 9 million hectares were cleared for pasture formation, more than 72 percent of the 12,365,000 hectares altered by 1980.

Small farmer settlements, many government-promoted, have been the second largest cause of deforestation. These sponsored programs, along with the skewed distribution of land tenure, agricultural mechanization, recurrent droughts, and economic depression, stimulated migration from other parts of the country. Huge government investments in roads and other infrastructure, projected to total more than US$6.2 billion by 1990 (Hecht 1986) have contributed to the population growth rate in the Amazon of 6.13 percent per year, compared to a national average of 2.78 percent. In Rondônia, the site of the government-sponsored POLONOROESTE development pro-

Brazilian forests are home to as many as one fifth of the world's plant and animal species and contain nearly one third of the world's broad-leafed timber, an estimated 48 to 78 million cubic meters with a market value of as much as US$1.7 trillion (at 1984 prices).

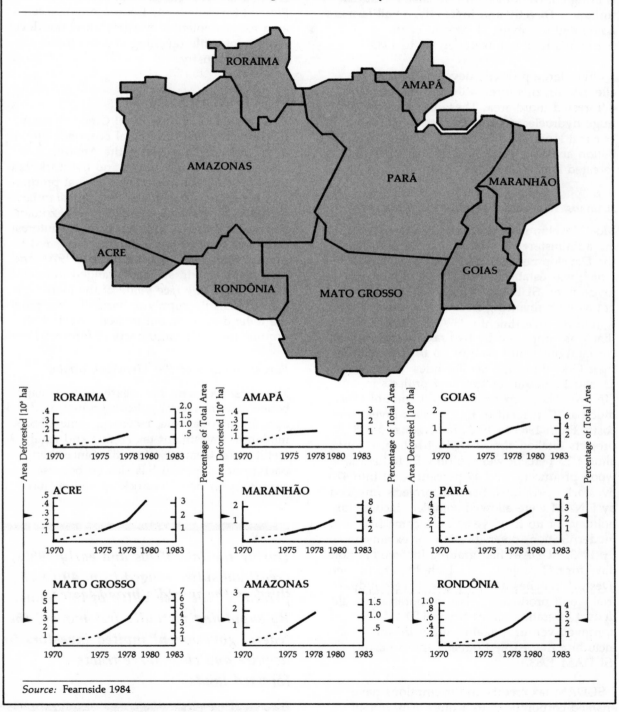

Figure II.E.1. Tendencies in the Rate of Increase of Forest Cover Alteration in Legal Amazonia (Area Deforested as Percentage of Total Area by State)

Source: Fearnside 1984

75

gram, population grew at a staggering 34.2 percent annual rate. Many settlers practiced shifting cultivation, with extensive forest disturbance. Directly and indirectly, small farmers accounted for about 11 percent of the Amazon's total deforestation up to 1983.

Other large projects, developed partly to alleviate Brazil's foreign debt crisis, have deforested more area. These include several huge hydroelectric investments, such as the Tucurui Hydroelectric Project, which cost US$4 billion and flooded 2160 square kilometers of forested land. (Goodland 1985: 6.)

Amazon Regional Development Policies

Most development programs in the Amazon are administered by the Superintendency for the Development of the Amazon (SUDAM), which was established in 1966 to attract private investment. SUDAM established incentive programs with financing from an investment fund, Fundo de Investimento da Amazônia (FINAM), that was supported by two tax subsidies. First, corporations could exempt up to 50 percent of their federal income tax liabilities by investing an equal amount for specified projects in FINAM. These tax credits could amount to as much as 75 percent of total project investment costs. From 1965 to 1983, tax credits to 808 projects totalled almost US$1.4 billion. Of this, almost 35 percent went to only 59 industrial wood producers, and 42 percent went into 470 livestock operations. Second, projects financed by FINAM were allowed complete income tax holidays of up to 15 years on income from modernization, diversification, or expansion. By 1983, SUDAM had granted income tax holidays for 843 projects, of which 39 percent were livestock ranches and 31 percent were industrial wood producers. Also, corporations could deduct operating losses from SUDAM-approved ventures against other income, including that earned outside the Amazon. (SUDAM 1983.)

SUDAM tax credits and exemptions have enabled corporations to acquire Amazonian projects for a fraction of actual development costs. In 1980, approximately 24,000 companies claimed tax deductions from investments in FINAM in 1980 alone. Tax incentives accelerated forest depletion by stimulating the development of cattle ranching and the forest products industry.

Rural Credit System

The Brazilian National Rural Credit System, developed to stimulate rural economic growth in such priority regions as the Amazon, has offered loans to agriculture and livestock ventures for capital investments, annual production operations, and marketing. Substantial subsidies have been provided to Amazonian borrowers through 12-percent annual interest rates and six-year grace periods compared to 45 percent elsewhere. During the late 1970s and early 1980s, credit subsidies ranged from 49 to 76 percent of the face value of the loans. *(See Table II.E.1.)* By supplying virtually free money, the federal government invited investors to acquire and clear large tracts of forested lands.

Forest Impacts of the Livestock Sector

The livestock sector has clearly been a major beneficiary of federal policies promoting development in Amazonia, receiving some US$730 million in investment tax credits and rural credit loans from 1966 to 1983. Since then, pasture development has slowed because approvals for new livestock operations have

---

During the late 1970s and early 1980s, credit subsidies ranged from 49 to 76 percent of the face value of the loans. By supplying virtually free money, the federal government invited investors to acquire and clear large tracts of forested lands.

Table II.E.1. Rural Credit Subsidy Rates 1975–81

	1975	1976	1977	1978	1979	1980	1981
Commercial Interest Rate[a]	34.6	34.4	41.1	36.4	44.8	59.4	77.6
Rural Credit Interest Rate[b]	12.0	12.0	12.0	12.0	12.0	12.0	12.0
Effective Rural Interest Rate[c]	5.0	5.0	5.0	5.0	5.0	5.0	5.0
Percentage of Interest Rate Subsidized[d]	86%	86%	88%	86%	89%	92%	94%
Interest Rate Subsidy Relative to Credit Amount[e]	49%	49%	56%	51%	59%	69%	76%

Notes:
a. Rate of return on Brazilian treasury bonds, corrected for changes in CPI and monetary correction. Source: IMF 1983.
b. Interest rate of PROTERRA loans to borrowers in Legal Amazonia.
c. The internal rate of return equivalent to a credit on PROTERRA terms.
d. The difference between the commercial and effective rural interest rates, expressed as a percentage of the commercial interest rate.
e. One minus the present value of debt service payments on PROTERRA loans (calculated at the commercial interest rate as discount factor), divided by the initial loan value.

been curtailed and Brazil has suffered an economic depression. Of the various subsidy recipients, SUDAM-supported livestock projects have had the greatest impact on forest reserves, accounting for 20 percent of the total deforestation recorded by Landsat monitoring from 1973 to 1983. SUDAM projects tend to be more depression-proof than other ventures because of long-term financing, tax holidays, provisions for loss write-offs for up to 15 years, and access to several investment tax credits for a single project. SUDAM ranches are also much larger than unsponsored ones, averaging over 22,000 hectares versus only 9,300 hectares. (Pompermayer 1979.) As a result, most future forest clearance for pasture will take place on the land still available on these SUDAM-sponsored ranches.

Financial Performance of Subsidized Amazon Cattle Ranches

The Brazilian government's support for livestock projects in the Amazon has been founded on their potential to stimulate long-term economic development. However, analyses of typical SUDAM-supported cattle ranches reveal that they are inherently uneconomic. Private investors have typically realized profits only through tax and rural credit subsidies. The government has financed not only losses

Table II.E.2. Cost Structure and Returns on Typical SUDAM Beef Cattle Ranch (US$ per hectare during five-year development period)

CAPITAL INVESTMENT	1984	FIVE-YEAR OPERATING COSTS	1984
1. Land Cost	31.70	1. Labor Costs[c]	26.16
2. Forest Clearance Manual	65.95	2. Herd Management[d]	21.00
3. Pasture Planting	26.36	3. Pasture Maintenance[e]	47.34
4. Fencing	19.38	4. Facility Maintenance[f]	74.35
5. Road-building[a]	6.31	5. Administration[g]	4.11
6. Miscellaneous Constructions	1.25		
7. Cattle Acquisition[b]	90.87		
Sub-Total	241.82	Sub-Total	173.00
TOTAL COSTS	414.78	TOTAL REVENUES[h]	112.50

Notes:
a. Road-building: Based on US$676.20 per kilometer as given by seven rancher respondents and average of 108 kilometers per ranch divided by average pasture area (11,600 hectares). The average size of the ranches in the sample was 49,500 hectares.
b. Cattle acquisition: Based on total initial herd of 4,000 animals costing US$1,054,300 on 11,600 hectares of pasture.
c. Labor costs: Based on 52 permanent employees per ranch and an average annual payroll of US$60,500 and 11,600 hectares of pasture, as provided by 24 rancher respondents.
d. Herd maintenance: Based on annual animal vaccination costing US$2.50 per hectare and mineral salts costing US$1.70 per hectare, totaling US$4.20 per year.
e. Pasture maintenance: Based on two pasture cleanings (US$10.49 per hectare) and one replanting (US$26.36 per hectare) totaling US$47.34 during the five-year period.
f. Facility maintenance (roads, fences, corrals, buildings, etc.): Based on US$14.87 per hectare per year as given by 10 rancher respondents.
g. Administration: Based on 10 percent of capital investment and five-year operating costs.
h. Revenues: Based on observed take-off rate of 17.1 percent in 1984 (1,026 fattened steers/year), and an average 1984 price of US$254.37 per head as given by 12 rancher respondents or a total of US$260,983 (US$112.50 per hectare) per five-year and pasture of 11,600 hectares.

Source: Browder 1985.

in the projects themselves, but also the profits supplied to private entrepreneurs.

The cost structure and returns for a typical SUDAM-supported cattle ranch are shown in Table II.E.2.

An economic and financial analysis based on these parameters show the divergence between private and public rewards. *(See Table II.E.3)* The analysis assumes that land, cattle, and equipment are sold at the end of the 15-year investment period; that inflation averages 25 percent annually, approximating levels of the 1970s; that land values rise at 2 percent per year above the inflation rate; and that the real interest rate is at 5 percent.

Table II.E.3. Economic and Financial Analysis of Government-Assisted Cattle Ranches in the Brazilian Amazon

	Net Present Value (US$)	Total Investment Outlay (US$)	NPV: Investment Outlay
I. Economic analysis			
A. Base case	−2,824,000	5,143,700	−.55
B. Sensitivity analysis			
1. Cattle prices assumed doubled	511,380	5,143,700	+.10
2. Land prices assumed rising 5%/yr. more than general inflation rate	−2,300,370	5,143,700	−.45
II. Financial analysis			
A. Reflecting all investor incentives: tax credits, deductions, and subsidized loans	1,875,400	753,650	+2.49
B. Sensitivity analysis			
1. Interest rate subsidies eliminated	849,000	753,650	+1.13
2. Deductibility of losses against other taxable income eliminated	−658,500	753,650	−0.87

In the base case, the net present value of the venture is a loss of US$2.8 million, 55 percent of the total investment. Sensitivity analysis reveals that the project would still lose some US$2.3 million, or 45 percent of the initial investment, if land values increased at 5 percent per year above the inflation rate. Only a doubling of cattle prices above those observed in the base case would make the operation marginally economic, providing a return of US$0.5 million, or 10 percent.

Because of the subsidies provided, however, these uneconomic projects have been extremely lucrative for the private entrepreneur able to use all available incentives. The financial analysis summarized in the second panel of Table II.E.3 embodies the same parameters and assumptions, but in accordance with underlying survey data, it assumes that tax credits are used to finance 54 percent of investment

Government subsidies have been the driving force behind large private investments in livestock ventures in Amazonian forests.

costs. Of the remaining 46 percent, half is borrowed through rural credit loans and the rest is supplied by the investor. The discounted present value of net returns to the investor in a typical ranch is US$1.87 million, nearly 2.5 times the investor's equity, even though the ranch itself loses money. Sensitivity analysis showed that if interest rate subsidies were removed, the discounted present value would be reduced to US$0.85 million, a 13 percent return on the investor's equity. If deductions of operating losses against other taxable income are also eliminated, the project produces a loss to the investor of US$0.65 million. Clearly, government subsidies have been the driving force behind large private investments in livestock ventures in the Amazon.

The opportunity cost of merchantable timber lost during forest clearance is another economic cost of these projects. Only 20 percent of all SUDAM-supported operations ever marketed their timber, (in contrast to 47 percent of non-subsidized ranches) because investors had other easy sources of finance and wanted to clear the forests quickly to prove their eligibility for government programs.

The value of lost timber appears to have been significant. On an average SUDAM ranch of 22,500 hectares, about 5,500 hectares have been cleared for pastures. With an average density of merchantable roundwood equivalent of 24 cubic meters per hectare, this amounts to about 132,000 cubic meters per ranch. If only 20 percent of the 470 SUDAM projects in operation in 1983 marketed their timber, then some 375 did not. This equates to a potential loss of nearly 50,000,000 cubic meters of roundwood.

At conservative estimates of 1985 stumpage values for commercial species other than mahogany ranging from US$2 to US$5 per cubic meter, the opportunity cost from lost timber totals US$100 to US$250 million, one eighth to one third of all SUDAM tax credits distributed to Amazonian livestock ventures from 1966 to 1983.

Small Farmer Settlement Policies and the Forest Sector

Although not as extensive as efforts to promote large-scale private investment in the Amazon, government-sponsored settlements of small farmers have also influenced regional development and related forest depletion. The National Integration Program (PIN), established in 1970, was the government's first major attempt to integrate the Amazon region with Brazil's "economic mainland." The program was based on massive highway construction as the means for opening up the Amazon to agricultural development by the rural masses. Two main highways, the east-west Transamazon and the north-south Cuiaba-Santarem, were proposed to bisect the region. Lands adjacent to these roads were to be settled by small farmers, with villages and cities interspersed at regular intervals.

Initial plans projected the relocation of 100,000 families onto 100 hectare lots by 1976. Due mainly to bureaucratic inefficiencies and poor planning, only 12,800 families were settled by 1978 (Bunker 1985), and plans for creating urban centers to supply infrastructure also failed to materialize. (Pompermayer 1979.) Difficulties in maintaining access on the Transamazon highway, especially during the rainy season, restricted transportation and communication. Most important, livestock interest groups influenced the government to shift its policy focus back to large-scale private development.

Before being essentially abandoned in 1975, the National Integration Program was an expensive effort for the Brazilian government. Highway construction cost an estimated US$120 million, while urban development required an additional US$11.5 million. (Moran 1976: 81.) The direct costs of relocating and settling families totaled US$103 million (about US$13,000 per family). However, total costs, including housing, an initial salary, local social overhead, and administration, were nearly US$39,000 per person.

The program was environmentally costly as well. As much as 640,000 hectares of tropical forest may have been directly converted to agriculture by the new farmers. This amounts to almost 15 percent of the total deforestation recorded in Para, where most PIN settlements were concentrated, and 4.3 percent of the forest alteration recorded by 1983 for the entire Amazon region.

The other major government-sponsored colonization program, which has been the focus of much international attention, is the Northwest Brazil Integrated Development Program (POLONOROESTE). Established in 1981, the program was the first attempt to fully coordinate development in Rondônia and western Mato Grosso, where spontaneous settlement had been ongoing for decades. As with the PIN, POLONOROESTE has also been based on extensive road construction, with nearly US$570 million allocated for work on the Cuiba-Porto Velho highway. (World Bank 1981: 1.) Under the POLONOROESTE program, settlers get no stipend and must pay moving and forest clearance expenses by selling the timber they remove, so total costs for the program average "only" US$17,000 per household.

At least some consideration has been given to the indigenous people and biologically rich sites in the area affected by the POLONOROESTE project. Forty-six reserves totaling 5.1 million hectares have been granted protection. (Myers 1984.) This represents 21 percent of Rondônia, which is endowed with one of the world's richest and most diverse ecosystems. Nevertheless, by 1983, some 990,000 hectares of forested land had been converted by resettled farmers, an area equal to 71 percent of the total deforestation recorded in Rondônia at that time, and 6.7 percent of the 14.8 million hectares of forests lost in the entire Amazon region.

Substantial land grants provided by the PIN and POLONOROESTE programs have contributed further to the loss of the Amazon's forest resources. Land with a market value of nearly US$32 per hectare has been offered at only US$1 per hectare. Thus, settlers get an implicit subsidy totaling US$163 million in Rondônia alone, or US$3,200 per person. By obtaining titles to such cheap and readily available land, many colonists have become eligible for loans under the rural credit system. In Rondónia, 49 percent of the settlers holding titles in 1985 had borrowed at least once for agricultural or livestock projects. Of these, 61 percent cleared more land than the average area

cleared by all farmers. Subsidized settlers cleared almost 25 percent more forests than those not benefitting from government programs.

In Brazil, most of the extensive deforestation of the Amazon, totalling over 15 million hectares by 1987, can be traced directly to government-financed programs and subsidies. The fiscal burden has been heavy, the environmental consequences serious, and the contribution to Brazilian development dubious at best.

West Africa

Forest Resources and Deforestation

Since 1975, the disappearance rate of West Africa's productive closed forest has been the world's highest. Liberia, Ghana, the Ivory Coast, and Gabon account for nearly all African exports of tropical hardwood products. In three of the four, deforestation has been extremely rapid.

Liberia. Centuries ago, shifting cultivators removed the primary forest cover. After disease, slavery, and tribal warfare reduced the population in the 1700s, the low bush in abandoned areas recovered into today's high secondary forest. Liberia is now undergoing a second round of deforestation that has doubled its pace in the past 40 years. (FAO 1986: 276.) Shifting cultivation, primarily for upland rice, is the principal cause. Cultivators encroach on logged-over forests, so the many logging roads built since 1963 have made once-remote areas easily accessible to slash-and-burn farmers.

Virtually no private forest property rights are recognized in Liberia. Government-owned national forests comprise nearly the entire forest area. In them, shifting cultivation is illegal, but prohibitions are not well enforced. (FAO 1986: 277.)

Ghana. Here too, the tropical forests have long been suffering depletion. In 1900, natural forests covered one third of the country; by 1980, virgin forest had all but vanished. (Sutlive 1981: 111.) Deforestation slowed after 1980 mainly because little forest was left.

Poverty-driven shifting cultivation and fuelwood harvests have been the principal causes, but logging and conversion of closed forest areas to permanent tree crops, particularly cocoa, also played a role. Both plantations and logging receded as causes of deforestation after 1960, but new logging roads have still helped spread shifting cultivation.

Poverty-driven deforestation resulted from Ghana's economic decline since independence in 1957. As the number of impoverished families rose dramatically starting in 1970, both the area under shifting cultivation and fuelwood consumption grew rapidly. Fuelwood cutting accelerated sharply after the mid-1970s; by 1983, Ghana's per capita fuelwood consumption was one of the world's highest, and it is still rising rapidly. The fuelwood harvest is about 12 times the volume of logs harvested for wood products. (FAO 1986.)

Changes in property rights have also affected the rate of deforestation. Usufruct rights over forest resources were originally those of customary law. In the early 1970s, as an outgrowth of political conflict, all rights over natural right were stripped from the traditional communities and assumed by the central government. As a result, Ghanaian forests are now even more vulnerable to the "tragedy of the commons" than they were when property rights were vested in tribal groups, which had some incentive to maintain the resource. The transfer of all forest rights to the national

Ghanaian forests are now even more vulnerable to the "tragedy of the commons" than they were when property rights were vested in tribal groups, which had some incentive to maintain the resource.

government has meant that access to the remaining forest is virtually unchecked.

Ivory Coast. The Ivory Coast has experienced the most rapid deforestation of any country since the mid-1950s. (Simon and Kahn, 1980: 160–161.) The average annual deforestation rate, as a percent of the remaining forest, rose from 2.4 percent in 1956–1965 to 7.3 percent in 1981–1985, over ten times the world average rate of 0.6 percent.

The principal causes have been shifting cultivation, logging, and agro-conversion. Rapid population growth, a consequence of high fertility and a very high rate of immigration from low-income neighboring countries, has expanded shifting cultivation. [FAO(B) 1981: 124–125.] Here too it is difficult to assess the relative roles of logging and shifting cultivation because shifting cultivators have moved into areas opened up by logging. Agro-conversion to cocoa and coffee estates has also been significant but its effect, relative to shifting cultivation, is unclear. (Spears 1986: 4.)

Gabon. Gabon is atypical. First, Gabon was not a poor country even in the 1960s and 1970s, so shifting cultivation has probably contributed little to deforestation. (World Bank 1985: 232.) Second, much of the nation's tropical forest remains undisturbed. Seventy-seven percent of total land area is still covered with dense forest, and recent deforestation rates are among the lowest in Africa. Third, the Gabonese forest sector is still dominated by foreign enterprises. Fourth, Gabonese taxes and forest fees are among the lowest in the tropical world. Fifth, Gabon, unlike most other major producers of tropical timber, has not promoted domestic wood processing. Finally, Gabon was the first tropical African nation to enact a reforestation tax. (Sutlive 1981: 162.)

Inaccessibility rather than public policy has limited deforestation, although Gabon has set aside fairly large forest areas as national parks. (Myers 1985: 37.) As transportation improves with the spread of the Trans-Gabon Railway and as tropical forests are depleted elsewhere in Africa, Gabon's tropical forest resources will face the same pressures as the Ivory Coast and Ghana did.

Property rights in Gabon strongly resemble those in the other African countries. The forestry code distinguishes among the property rights of the state, individuals, and tribal groups, but the state holds virtually all property rights. [FAO(B) 1981: 272.]

Foreign Investment

Liberia. Liberia's forestry sector has attracted foreign capital for almost four decades. In 1975, three of the five timber companies operating in Liberia were foreign owned. Thereafter, the number of timber companies expanded through 1983, as did the share of foreign owned firms in exports. Most sawmills were also foreign owned: in 1980, of 20 sawmills surveyed 16 were foreign owned and accounted for 85 percent of capacity. Growth in foreign investment slowed after 1980, when a military coup ended decades of relative political stability. (World Bank 1985: Table 2.)

Ghana. At independence the Ghanaian timber industry was dominated by large foreign corporations, and the new government tried to secure control by adopting such policies as preferential concessions and subsidies. In 1973, the government finally directed all multinational natural resource firms to surrender 55 percent of equity to the government. The four

multinationals remaining at that time sold their interests and left the Ghana timber industry.

Ivory Coast. Exploitation of the Ivorian forest by Europeans dates to the end of the 19th century when British and French interests began harvesting ebony logs. Activity grew slowly until the port of Abidjan was opened in 1951, after which the harvest of tropical hardwood logs increased spectacularly. Transnational corporations, mostly French, enjoyed a relatively free hand and established very large logging operations.

The Forestry Code of 1965 was designed primarily to induce foreign investors to build processing mills. Large concession areas and longer contract terms were reserved for firms willing to start processing. These incentives had little effect, since foreign investors continued to export the most desirable hardwoods as logs. (Arnaud and Sournia 1980: 295.) The government then limited exports of these species and linked new concession terms to the degree of industrialization, a step that also failed: the transnational corporations merely regarded the required investments as a relatively small added cost of log exports. The Ivory Coast still has one of the most laissez-faire forest policies in Africa. All operating rights are tradeable, for example, including subcontracting of concessions and export quotas.

Ivory Coast has one of the most laissez-faire forest policies in Africa.

Gabon. Although the first commercial export-oriented exploitation of the Gabonese forest began in 1905, large-scale harvesting did not occur until 1947 with the entry of a large French firm. Today, the country is divided into two zones: Zone 1, nearer the coast, is reserved for domestic firms with limited capital resources, while inland Zone 2 is available to foreign investors. Gabon is one of the few countries that still permits almost 100-percent foreign equity ownership in national resource projects. A few large firms are wholly French owned. Since 1970, however, all new entrants into Gabon must provide "free equity," usually 10 percent of total equity. (Gillis, Deprah and Mescher 1983: 4-8.)

Benefits and Rent Capture in Forest Exploitation Income, Employment, Exports and Tax Revenues

Liberia. Value added in the Liberian forest sector has been a rising proportion of relatively stagnant GDP since 1973. Between 1973 and 1980, employment in forestry grew from 1,200 persons to 5,900, and log exports increased at roughly the same pace as total log production.

Fiscal benefits from forest sector exploitation have not been substantial, but (at one-fifth total export value) are a larger fraction than in other West African nations. In the early 1980s, forest fees and forest taxes accounted for slightly less than 8 percent of total government revenues.

Ghana. The forest sector's contribution to GDP has been remarkably constant since 1965 at a value-added level of 6.2 percent. (Gillis et al. 1983: 4.) Given that GDP declined steadily from then until the present, the forest sector fared little worse than the rest of the ailing economy. Before 1965, timber exports furnished as much as 20 percent of total export earnings. By 1980, timber's share had fallen to 4 percent, even as the value of all exports declined steadily. Employment in forestry, however, did increase significantly from 1965 until 1979, when it peaked at 101,000 persons and then declined in 1982 to 70,000 persons.

Ivory Coast. The forest-based sector has played a larger role in the Ivorian economy than in any other African country. Value added in the forest sector, never lower than 5.6 percent of GDP, reached 8 percent in 1976, while the overall economy was growing rapidly. Since logs accounted for almost all the wood production, the forest sector has not created many jobs. Sectoral employment peaked at 24,000 in 1977 before declining to 15,000, almost the same level as in 1972.

During the 1970s, the forest sector furnished between 5.8 and 8.0 percent of total government revenues, much more than in any other African country save Liberia. Forest taxes and fees nearly 25 percent of export value in 1971, had by 1980 fallen to only 11 percent— anomalous since export tax rates were drastically increased throughout the 1970s. The duties on many high-value species in 1979 were 9 times their 1970 levels. The decline in the ratio of export taxes and fees to total export value is explained partly by the rising share of lightly taxed processed wood in timber exports and by a fall in the share of higher-valued species as richer stands were depleted.

Gabon. The forest sector accounted for 80 percent of exports as late as 1963, after which oil and uranium became the main sources of domestic value-added exports and tax revenues. The forest sector remains a major source of employment: 28 percent of the labor-force works in logging and wood processing activities, a higher percentage than in any other nation. However, the sector accounts for only one to two percent of fiscal revenues.

Rent Capture

Liberia. In the mid-1970s, Liberia had one of the least effective rent-capture policies among African timber exporting nations. *(See Table II.F.1.)* By 1979, after two major increases in forest fees, Liberia had set up a system that would capture about two thirds of the total rent available in logging if all taxes and charges were collected. (Peprah 1982.)

Before 1973, Liberia tailored tax terms to each investor. After 1973, Liberia developed a standard timber contract package: a five-year tax holiday, exemption of 20 percent of income

Table II.F.1. Liberia and Selected West African Nations: Logger's Residuals After Government Forest Tax and Transport Cost Deductions 1974 (selected species) US$ per m³

	Ivory Coast	Liberia	Cameroon[1]	Congo[2]	Gabon
High value species					
—Sapelli	46	80	51/42	76/64	78
—Sipo	47	98	72/63	86/74	100
Middle value species					
—Tiama	28	55	37/29	49/47	53
—Kossipo	38	63	33/24	56/44	61
—Iroko	26	55	27/16	50/35	49
Low value species					
—Llomba	9	25	13/ 5	22/11	20
—Fromager	25	25	15/ 8	24/15	23

1. Douala Route/Pointe Noire Route
2. Southern Sector (Mossendjo)/Northern Sector (Quesso)

Source: Schmithusen 1980.

Table II.F.2. Liberia: Theoretical Rent Capture in Logging 1979 (selected species) US$ per m³

	(1)	(2)			(3)	(4)	(5)
		A	B	C	Gross Margin	Total Taxes and Forest Fees (incl.	Total Govt. Revenue as % of Gross
	Sales Revenue	Logging Costs	Other Costs	Total Costs	(1) – (2)ᶜ for Logger	income tax)	margin (4) – (3)
Sapelli	187	67.30	12.95	80.25	106.75	71.11	66.7
Acajou	141	67.30	12.95	80.25	60.75	48.10	79.2
Sipo	254	67.30	12.95	80.25	173.75	114.62	66.0
Iroko	100	67.30	12.95	80.25	19.75	20.50	104.0
Tiama	155	67.30	12.95	80.25	74.75	55.11	73.7
Llomba	57	67.30	12.95	80.25	negative	9.5	—
Fromager	50	67.30	12.95	80.25	negative	7.5	—

Source: Peprah 1982.

from tax after the holiday period, and exemption from import duties on equipment, materials, and spare parts for five years. Other fiscal incentives offered in the 1970s included exemption from log-export duty, reduced severance fees, and exemption from petroleum taxes. Because national returns were exceedingly low under these terms, from 1977 royalties and fees were sharply increased and tax incentives curtailed. Tax holidays were abolished, customs duty exemptions were reduced from five to two years, and today all timber companies pay income tax at the maximum rate of 50 percent.

In 1977, the government enacted a severance fee for logs of all species, whether exported or used domestically. (Gray 1983: 87.) Such a uniform specific rate royalty causes high-grading of the timber stands but in Liberia the rate is not high enough to cause much damage. Still, the reforestation fee and other uniform fees further encourage high grading. As Table II.F.2 indicates, if all taxes and fees were actually collected, in 1979 loggers could not have afforded to harvest any low-value species and would have bypassed even some middle-valued species.

Ghana. Because of rampant smuggling, estimation of government capture of timber rents after 1975 is impossible. However, according to fairly reliable estimates for earlier years, rents averaged 26 percent of the value of log output in the early 1970s, but up to 80 percent for some particularly desirable species. Of the total timber rent, government royalties, taxes, marketing board charges, and corporate taxes captured only 38 percent. The logging industry kept more than three-fifths, and of this, 35 percent went to Ghanaian and 27 percent to foreign investors.

Over the post-independence era, royalty policies changed in stages. Now there is a specific royalty on trees harvested with a different rate for each species. Since the royalty is based on stems taken rather than volume, loggers might cut large trees that they otherwise would have by-passed had the royalty been based on volume per tree, and in this way provide much larger canopy openings for young saplings and less competition for nutrients. Loggers in Ghana do leave defective trees and nonmarketable species, but the effects of high-grading are not pronounced. This system ensures that many young trees will be left to form the next crop, and also encourages fuller use of cut trees. (Gray 1983: 131.) The Ghanaian royalty

structure merits consideration by other countries.

Unfortunately, in recent years the royalty system has not raised much forest revenue. Once Ghana's terribly overvalued currency was allowed to depreciate, forest royalties and fees fixed in terms of local currency became negligible in foreign exchange value.

Ivory Coast. Aggressive taxation during the 1970s enabled the Ivory Coast to capture a higher fraction of rents in timber than other West African countries. The rents retained by loggers for higher-value species were well below comparable residuals in Liberia and Gabon, and for middle-valued species retained rents were half those in other African nations except Cameroon.

Since 1980, the generally applicable rate of corporate income tax has been 40 percent, though firms may apply for special tax incentives. Firms with "priority" status may receive income tax holidays for 7 to 11 years and sometimes up to 15 years. Timber firms are also eligible for a special incentive whereby half of all amounts invested in government-approved programs may be immediately deducted from taxable income rather than depreciated over time. Much of the pressure for such tax incentives comes from French logging companies, which are not taxed by the French government on income earned overseas and therefore benefit greatly from income tax reductions.

Royalties are imposed on timber volume, not on trees cut, but are differentiated by species and destination: royalties on high-value species are three times those on low-value species and exported logs are subject to rates twice as high as those imposed on logs used locally. The fee level is too low to affect high-grading seriously. Licence and area fees are also collected from logging firms but are too low to influence harvest decisions. (World Bank 1986, Annex 5: 12.)

The export tax is the most significant forest

revenue source, accounting for about 90 percent of the total. The ad-valorem tax is based on the posted price of log exports, which have typically been slightly below actual f.o.b. prices. Rates for some of the principal species of exported logs ranged from a low of 24.6 percent of the low-value *Llomba* species to as high as 44.6 percent for the prized *Sipo*.

Gabon. Although Gabon's forest sector has been an important source of value-added, export earnings, and employment, it has not been a major source of tax revenues. in the mid-1970s, Gabonese policies toward rent capture were the weakest in Africa, and the timber sector continues to be one of the most lightly taxed in all of Africa, if not the world. Gabon collected only a felling tax of 5 percent of posted export value, which tends to be below realized f.o.b. values. It collects almost no

Gabonese policies toward rent capture were the weakest in Africa, and the timber sector continues to be one of the most lightly taxed in all of Africa, if not the world.

other taxes on forest products: there is no evidence of any licence or area fee. Gabonese export taxes are 20 percent of posted f.o.b. values for logs and 12 percent for sawntimber and other processed wood. Lower rates, averaging 10-11 percent apply to other species of logs and to processed products. Gabon thus provides a relatively mild export tax incentive for domestic processing compared to other countries. The corporation income tax rate in Gabon is imposed at a rate of 50 percent, but exemptions abound. The Gabon Investment Code allows all timber companies a two-year tax holiday plus a 50-percent remission of taxes in the third year. Firms are also exempted from various minor levies for five to ten years.

Concession Terms

Liberia. Until 1973, each concessionaire negotiated its own concession agreement so terms varied considerably. (Gray 1983: 195.) Concession agreements adopted in 1973 contained uniform standards for durations of contracts, logging practices, silvicultural treatment, and taxes. Concession contracts now run 25 years, not long enough to provide a clear incentive to maintain the productive value of the forest, but longer than in many other African countries. Harvest methods are restricted to selective cutting plans that promote natural regeneration and reduce high-grading by requiring the harvest of all primary trees with diameter of more than 40 cm and requiring the harvest of 30 percent of all standing stock composed of secondary species. Whether these rules have been enforced remains unclear.

Ghana. Prior to independence, timber firms in Ghana typically obtained concessions of 50 years with a few for as long as 99 years. (Page, Scott, Leland 1976: 26.) While 50 years should have been long enough to induce firms to practice sustained yield forestry, they did not do so. This suggests that longer concession periods mean little in the absence of complementary measures to curtail forest depletion. (Pearson and Page 1972.) Major changes in concessions policy were promulgated after 1971. Concessions were granted only to Ghanaians, and the average size of new concessions was sharply reduced. In addition the length of concessions was set at a minimum of five years and a maximum of 25 for areas exceeding 800 hectares and a maximum of three years for smaller areas. [FAO(B) 1981: 196.]

Ivory Coast. Most early forest concession contracts lasted only five years. In 1965–68, concessions were altered: five years for logging companies, ten years for companies operating sawmills and fifteen for integrated wood processing firms. Until 1972, harvest methods were not prescribed in the contracts. After 1972, firms were required to submit information on logging and road-construction programs, as well as on past operations. Short of staff, the forestry ministry did not require concessionaires to follow any particular selection or cutting method, and it imposed on the firms only girth limits for harvests.

Gabon. Forest concessions are granted for a minimum of 30 years for logging and even longer for a firm investing in local processing. Clearcutting is prohibited and harvesting is restricted to selective cutting.

Forest-based Industrialization Policies

Liberia. In the early 1970s, Liberia switched from a passive stance toward forest-based industrialization to one of the most aggressive in Africa. Two policies were introduced in 1977: a major increase in the Industrialization Incentive Fee (IIF) applied to log exports, and enactment of a Forest Products Fee (FPF) imposed on sawnwood exports. The IIF—the most important forest tax in terms of government revenues and impact on processing decisions—is levied on all exported logs at rates ranging from US$75 on very high-value species to US$2 to US$4 on low-value species. The FPF also differentiates among species as well as by the degree of domestic processing.

Ghana. Government policies to promote wood processing industries have relied on export tax incentives and log export quotas or bans. In 1979, all export taxes on sawn timber were abolished, an action that proved meaningless given the deep currency overvaluation. (*Ghana Timber Board* 1979: 7.) Export bans have never been fully enforced. Hence, neither policy did much to foster industrialization. Subsidized credit for indigenous investment in sawmills and plymills, and income tax incentives for investment in processing plants had far more impact. From 1957 through 1971, subsidized loans to Ghanaian citizens were for 25 years with nominal interest rates half as high as commercial rates, which were themselves below high inflation rates. Manufacturing firms, including sawmills and plymills, have been

In the early 1970s, Liberia switched from a passive stance toward forest-based industrialization to one of the most aggressive in Africa.

entitled to income tax rebates. These policies led to substantial investment by the late 1960s, but wood processing industries operate inefficiently. (Page 1984.)

Ivory Coast. Policies have been strongly geared toward forest-based industrialization, particularly since 1972. The three most important policy instruments used have been the export tax structure, quotas on log exports, and export subsidies based on the amount of value-added to manufactured products.

The average plywood conversion rate in Ivorian mills in 1980 was only 40 percent. (Pfeiffer 1980: 40–42.) Many of the processing mills are ''window-dressing industries'' established solely to meet government's requirement that all log exporters invest in processing facilities. The government has foregone potential taxes from log exports to promote additional value-added from processing. For example, in 1980, the value of log exports of *Iroko*, a high-value species, was US$170 per cubic meter. Additional domestic value-added from processing these logs into sawn timber would have been about US$25, but for each cubic meter of *Iroko* exported as sawn timber the government gave up US$52 in potential export taxes. (*See Table II.F.3.*)

Efforts to increase industrialization levels include export quotas and subsidies. Log exports were scheduled for a complete ban by 1976, but instead rights to export logs were restricted by quotas to firms owning processing facilities. By 1982, quotas were applied to companies on a case-by-case basis, but quotas were freely traded among firms. Besides export

Table II.F.3. Ivory Coast: Export Taxes and Incentives for Domestic Processing on Selected Major Species

Species	Additional Domestic Value-Added from Sawmilling US$ per m³	Export Taxes Foregone by Government on Sawn Timber Exports US$ per m³	Taxes Foregone as % of Increased Value-added
Iroko	25.50	52.00	204
Acajou	19.20	43.00	224
Llomba	9.24	10.00	108

quotas, the government provides export subsidies based on the amount of value-added in manufactured products.

Gabon. Gabon has no log export quotas or bans. It does require that all concessionaires with contract areas over 15,000 hectares deliver 55 percent of the harvest to the local timber-processing industry. The large share of logs in total wood exports suggests that this policy has not been strongly enforced. The low protection rates may be one of the reasons for the very high conversion ratios of Gabonese mills, which must be as efficient as possible to compete in world markets. (Pfeiffer 1980.)

Reforestation

Liberia. Noticeable reforestation began in 1971. Liberia's Forest Management Plan obligated concessionaires to reforest one acre for every 30,000 board feet of merchantable timber harvested or pay US$150 per acre not reforested.

Three different forest regeneration methods are used: natural regeneration, enrichment planting, and forest plantations. Enrichment planting (planting valuable indigenous species to supplement the natural growing stock) has not been widely practiced. Plantations of quick-growing exotics for making pulpwood have been widely established in past years.

Ghana. The Forestry Department's reforestation program has been severely constrained. Domestic funds for reforestation programs come from reforestation fees. Although stipulated in all leases, fees were apparently not collected outside forest reserves until 1976. No record shows that any of the substantial reforestation fee receipts collected over the last 20 years have been spent for replanting. Nor have laws requiring concessionaires to replant after harvest been well enforced. [FAO(B) 1981: 277.]

Ivory Coast. No special taxes or charges on timber production have ever been imposed to finance reforestation. All reforestation efforts have been concentrated in a government agency, mostly to ensure wood supplies for pulp and paper projects. From 1966 to 1982, less than 3,000 hectares were reforested per year, compared to an annual deforestation rate of 300,000 hectares.

Gabon. Since 1957, the Government has collected a reforestation tax, the sole source of finance for reforestation programs until 1965. After that, the funds were supplemented with a general budgetary appropriation but at levels insufficient to support extensive activities. As a result there was almost no deliberate reforestation from 1968 to 1975, though efforts increased in 1982, when the reforestation tax was increased.

The United States

The National Forest system includes 191 million acres, more than a quarter of all U.S. forest land. Before WWII, most timber extraction took place on the more accessible and high-quality stands owned by private industry. Since then, the national forests have provided a significant fraction of timber supplies, now about one third of the soft wood harvest. Demands on national forests for both timber and for such benefits as recreation have grown, leading to inevitable conflict over the Forest Service management policies. (Wilkinson and Anderson 1985.)

Since its creation in 1905, the Forest Service has sought to promote development by supplying timber, with little thought for its own profit. In fact, on Forest Service lands, appraised stumpage values are estimated to cover the buyer's costs of extracting, processing, and selling the wood at a reasonable profit. (Beuter 1985.) Laws passed early in this century have linked revenues from timber sales and support for local communities, road construction, and future forestry activities. Such linkages, as well as the interests of the timber purchasers, create budgetary and political incentives for continued timber operations even on marginal sites. (Johnson 1985.) Even though law requires the Forest Service to consider economic efficiency in its operation, many critics charge that Forest Service timber operations on marginal forest lands fall far short of recovering even their direct costs.

The debate centers around the concept of multiple use management. In 1960, the Multiple Use Sustained Yield Act codified the policy of sustaining the flow of all the various benefits obtained from the national forests. These very general guidelines allocated considerable discretion to the Forest Service. Subsequent laws such as the Wilderness Act of 1964 have restricted this multiple use mandate by setting aside wilderness areas. The Forest and Rangeland Renewable Resources Planning Act (RPA) of 1974 and the National Forest Management Act of 1976, while confirming the Forest Service's multiple use management mandate, also tried to restrict timber operations on lands unfit for timber production. According to provision 6(k) of the 1976 Act, forest land economically or physically unsuitable for profitable timber investments should be segregated before management plans are formulated. So far, however, the Forest Service has not fully complied with that directive. Instead, it still manages all forests physically suitable for timber production under flexible multiple use criteria, deriving harvest plans for each area based on timber harvest targets. Production targets determine the areas deemed economically suitable for harvesting, not the reverse. (USDA 1986.)

Evaluating Below-Cost Timber Sales

Although timber production is a long-term investment, Forest Service accounts were not designed to compare costs and revenues over time. A national forest account for a particular year includes receipts from previous sales and costs incurred for future sales. They neither accumulate past expenses with interest, nor discount future benefits to a common base year. To make matters more complex, national forest management operations yield joint costs and benefits. Forest roads, for example, provide access to both loggers and recreational users. On Congressional instructions, the Forest Service in 1987 was designing an accounting system more appropriate for comparing costs and benefits of timber operations.

The Forest Service argues that timber operations that apparently lose money can be economic when non-timber benefits are taken into account, because of joint costs and benefits. The optimal management plan that maximizes the total net benefits over time could, in theory, cause continuous revenue losses on timber operations if harvests mainly supported non-timber objectives. (Scheuter and Jones 1985.)

Such optimization theory provides little practical guidance, however, since forest operations' effects on wildlife habitat, recreation, soil erosion, and water quality are often sharply debated and poorly estimated. Therefore, evaluations of forest operation have concentrated on tests of incremental efficiency. Such tests hold non-timber benefits constant and ask whether alternatives to proposed harvest plans that reduce timber harvests would reduce costs more than revenues. The test thereby separates out costs linked to non-timber benefits and evaluates only those directly attributable to timber-production activities. (Krutilla and Bower in press.) This test is still difficult, because accounts cannot fully separate costs of non-timber outputs from those of timber operations alone.

Some costs, such as those of road construction, jointly contribute to benefits over time and would ideally be allocated across current and future timber sales over the useful lifetimes of the roads. Several studies have taken this approach. (Hyde 1981; Hyde and Krutilla 1979; Helfand; Scheuter and Jones 1985; Minckler 1985; GAO 1984.) All but one found that where current sales involving road investments were unprofitable, future harvests and sales would also be unprofitable despite previous road construction. Once mature timber is harvested, the net present value of future rotations on unproductive sites is usually negative.

On a broader scale, four major studies, although limited by inadequate data, have investigated the incremental efficiency of forest operations, using somewhat different methodologies but arriving at remarkably similar conclusions.

1. The 1985 Congressional Research Service Estimates

This study examined both the net cash flows to the U.S. Treasury and a measure of net economic benefits of all timber sales in six western forest service regions in 1981 and 1982. (Beuter 1985.) *(See Table II.G.1.)*

The study had one major limitation: it focused on sales results in a period when timber prices were depressed. Partially offsetting this bias, the study used only winning bid amounts instead of eventual sales receipts, which are usually lower when prices are falling. To test incremental net revenues, the study adjusted certain accounting assumptions: payments to counties were defined not as costs to the federal government but as revenue transfers; and only roads financed by appropriated funds were included as incremental harvest costs.

Of the six western regions examined, the Pacific Southwest (region 5) and the Northwest (region 6) account for most of the revenues and profits. In the Southwest and Northern regions, net receipts were positive for both comparison years, though by narrower margins. Timber operations in the Rocky Mountain (region 2) and Intermountain belt (region 4) clearly do not cover direct costs. Even if road costs are omitted, net receipts fall far short of the costs of sale preparation, administration, and support in entire regions, even though these aggregates combine below-cost and above-cost operations.

Even if road costs are omitted, net receipts fall far short of the costs of sale preparation, administration, and support in entire regions, even though these aggregates combine below-cost and above-cost operations.

---

2. The 1984 General Accounting Office Estimates

The GAO study examined data on over 3,000 individual timber sales in 1981 and 1982 for regions 1,2,4 and 6. (GAO 1984.) Although sales receipts rather than winning bids were

Table II.G.1. Estimated Costs and Returns from Western Timber Sales 1981 and 1982 (US$ million)

	Northern	Rocky Mtn.	South Western	Inter-Mtn.	Pacific S.W.	Pacific N.W.
	1981					
CASH BIDS	75.5	4.8	43.5	4.8	319.4	1,335.0
Road Cost to Govt.	3.1	2.4	0.8	6.8	2.9	2.3
Sale Preparation and Administration	18.5	7.5	6.2	4.7	26.5	54.3
Pre-Sale and Support Costs	6.8	3.6	1.8	2.3	12.2	41.1
TOTAL DIRECT COSTS	28.4	13.5	8.8	13.8	41.6	97.7
NET REVENUES	47.1	−8.7	34.7	−9.0	277.8	1,237.3
	1982					
CASH BIDS	43.5	2.1	14.8	3.2	99.8	414.7
Road Cost to Govt.	6.8	1.0	1.4	4.9	7.5	11.5
Sale Preparation and Administration	16.4	6.3	4.9	4.0	25.2	41.8
Pre-Sale and Support Costs	10.6	5.4	2.5	3.5	20.4	55.6
TOTAL DIRECT COSTS	33.8	12.7	8.8	12.4	53.1	108.9
NET REVENUES	9.7	−10.6	6.0	−9.2	46.7	305.8

Source: Beuter 1985: 93.

used, the findings are similar to those of the CRS study. Despite methodological limitations, the results reproduced in Table II.G.2 indicate that over 90 percent of sales in regions 2 and 4 generated revenues insufficient to recover direct costs, while sales in region 6 generate large net revenues, and those in region 1 are mixed. The GAO study also examined a number of individual sales to explore why losses occurred and found the main cause to be timbering unproductive stands of low-valued species on difficult terrain with high harvesting costs. GAO data did not support the Forest Service's explanation that losses were incurred to open up promising areas for logging by building roads or to replant areas with higher valued, more productive stands.

3. The 1984 Congressional Research Service Estimates

A second CRS study gave a longer time perspective on timber revenues by examining forest-by-forest receipts between 1973 and 1983,

Table II.G.2. National Forest Timber Sales: Regions 1, 2, 4 and 6. Summary of Gains and Losses for Fiscal Years 1981 and 1982 (US$ thousands)

	1981				1982			
	Sales Showing Gains		Sales Showing Losses		Sales Showing Gains		Sales Showing Losses	
Region	No. of Sales	Amount of Gain	No. of Sales	Amount of Gain	No. of Sales	Amount of Gain	No. of Sales	Amount of Loss
1	135	$ 12,955	132	$19,016	74	$ 3,691	169	$26,220
2	5	51	75	14,117	1	3	73	13,860
4	8	86	62	13,450	3	3	73	10,422
6 (pine)	211	106,539	108	12,332	142	26,976	145	20,634
6 (Douglas fir)	838	597,624	56	5,097	717	121,237	217	21,639
TOTAL	1,197	$717,255	433	$64,012	937	$151,910	677	$92,775

Source: GAO 1984.

Table II.G.3. Acreage of National Forests that Consistently Record Below-Cost Sales and Total National Forest Acreage by Region

Region	(A) Regional Total of Below-Cost Acres	(B) Regional Total of National Forest System	(A/B) Percent
1	16,635,405	24,017,177	69
2	19,802,858	19,918,565	100
3	14,415,525	20,427,109	71
4	28,773,082	31,087,119	93
5	5,345,722	19,769,805	27
6	—	24,356,651	0
8	6,149,641	12,494,241	49
9	10,907,512	11,412,905	96
10	23,043,437	23,043,437	100
TOTAL	125,073,182	186,527,009	67

averaging out yearly fluctuations. (Wolf 1984.) The study also provided alternative estimates of separable costs: a minimum estimate of timber sale administration and resource support, and a broader estimate that also included tim-

ber stand improvement and timber roads financed by appropriated funds. When revenues deflated to 1982 prices were compared to these costs, a pattern similar to the other studies emerged.

4. Natural Resources Defense Council (NRDC) and Wilderness Society Estimates

Aggregate estimates for states or regions combine sales figures with positive or negative net revenues and hence underestimate the extent of below-costs sales. To alleviate this bias, the NRDC and the Wilderness Society examined costs and revenues for each national forest. (Barlow et al.; Sample 1984.) As Table II.G.3. shows, all national forests in Alaska, the Rocky Mountain and Intermountain regions show losses over the whole period. None of those in the Pacific Northwest do. In the East, almost all national forests consistently lose money on timber sales.

Upward and Downward Biases in the Estimates

The data on these issues are imprecise, so weighing the likely effects of biases in the estimates is important. Some potential biases may underestimate the net incremental benefits of timber operations. First, allocating costs to timber accounts that enhance non-timber objectives may bias net timber benefits downwards. In many Rocky Mountain, Intermountain, and Alaskan forests, however, timber operations fail efficiency tests by large margins even when minimal definitions of separable costs are adopted. Second, treating road costs as a current expense rather than amortizing it over timber operations during its useful life may add a downward bias. Studies often find, however, that even when road costs are omitted altogether, many forests fail incremental efficiency tests. Also, since road outlays have been steady over time in constant dollars and are projected at the same level, current outlays about equal annual road amortization charges.

A less obvious potential downward bias is buried in the appraisal system. If the Forest Service underestimates the current market value in its appraisal for a sale to a single bidder, who typically pays the appraised value, then the bidder receives a windfall. Forest Service statistical equations based on sale characteristics and past competitive bids show that appraised values are consistently low. This pattern has significant implications when 25 percent of total sales between 1973 and 1979 had one bidder, and within regions where most below-cost sales occur (those other than regions 5, 6 and 8) over 40 percent of the sales had only one bidder. Noncompetitive bidding based on appraised values well below market values contributes to Forest Service revenue losses, but also underestimates the net economic benefits of timber operation.

> *Twenty-five percent of total sales between 1973 and 1979 had one bidder, and within regions where most below-cost sales occur (those other than regions 5, 6 and 8) over 40 percent of the sales had only one bidder.*

A potential offsetting upward bias can be found in the cross subsidization of individual sales. The Forest Service often combines within one sale timber that can profitably be sold with timber that could not be sold if offered by itself. The Forest Service adjusts the appraised value of the profitable stands downward so that it can raise the apraised value of the unprofitable timber to the legal base rates. This practice allows bidders to meet or exceed appraised values and still make a profit on the sale as a whole. The larger sale justifies extending the road network and also increases the deposits retained on a larger timber volume, but the total costs of the sale go up, and the net returns to the treasury are much lower. In some cases, the Forest Service procedure amounts to paying the successful bidder to haul away unsalable timber. (USDA 1985: I-4.)

An analysis of this cross-subsidization showed that fully 40 percent of all timber sold

Table II.G.4. Values, Costs and Associated Outputs for Fiscal Year 1984 Timber Sale Program (US$ millions)[1] by Region

	Region				
	(1)	(2)	(3)	(4)	(5)
	Northern	Rocky Mountain	South Western	Inter-Mountain	Pacific Southwest
Value of Products Sold[2]	24.0	4.7	8.5	5.8	88.7
Associated Non-Timber Values[3]	28.5	14.1	13.3	10.1	31.9
Wildlife & Fish	(15.1)	(6.8)	(6.4)	(4.7)	(14.9)
Recreation	(13.1)	(6.9)	(6.2)	(5.0)	(16.6)
Range	(0.2)	(0.1)	(0.1)	(0.1)	(0.2)
Fuelwood	(0.1)	(0.3)	(0.6)	(0.3)	(0.2)
Production Costs[4]	35.1	12.3	12.3	14.2	62.0
Net (value less cost)	17.4	6.5	9.5	1.7	58.6
Roads[5]	45.4	19.8	13.3	14.2	48.4

Notes

1. Data are for National Forests and Grasslands only. Does not include regional office or Washington office costs.
2. This is the value of sawntimber, pulp, poles, and miscellaneous products such as posts, fuelwood, and Christmas trees. It does not include road values (purchaser credit or purchaser elected roads) or brush disposal, but does include K-V and salvage sale fund collections. The total value sold includes nonconvertible product value (approx. US$1.6 million) and the value of the long-term sale volume released (approx. US$1.1 million). These values are not included in the tables.
3. These represent total quantities of selected outputs associated with the annual timber program, based on constant per million board feet relationships in the 1985 RPA data base, current management alternative. These are the best estimates of field managers. Values per unit of output are based on those published in Table F.2, adjusted to 1984 terms, of the

in the western regions in 1983 was appraised to have a negative stumpage value. Comparing total revenue on these sales, with the appraised value of the more valuable species if sold alone estimates the revenue loss conservatively, since winning bids often exceed Forest Service appraisals and there is also cross-subsidization within sales of a single species. Nonetheless, the estimates show that in 1983 timber harvests could have been reduced by as much as 40

TABLE II.G.4. Continued

	Region				
	(6)	(8)	(9)	(10)	
	Pacific Northwest	Southern	Eastern	Alaska	TOTAL
Value of Products Sold[2]	333.7	76.9	19.2	1.7	563.2
Associated Non-Timber Values[3]	124.8	27.1	19.7	11.7	281.2
Wildlife & Fish	(59.6)	(12.5)	(8.2)	(5.7)	(133.9)
Recreation	(64.1)	(13.8)	(11.3)	(5.9)	(142.9)
Range	(0.8)	(0.1)	(0.1)	(—)	(1.7)
Fuelwood	(0.3)	(0.7)	(0.1)	(0.1)	(2.7)
Production Costs[4]	122.1	39.4	21.8	11.7	330.9
Net (value less cost)	336.4	64.6	17.1	1.7	513.5
Roads[5]	101.9	90.6	24.5	25.1	33.2

Notes continued

   Draft Environment Impact Statement for 1985 Resources Planning Act Program, except free-use fuelwood which is estimated annually by field managers. A Forest Service task force is currently studying the assignment of such associated outputs, costs, and benefits to the timber program.

4. These are National Forest costs of producing sawntimber, pulp, poles, and miscellaneous products. This includes timber management planning, silvicultural examination, sale preparation, harvest administration, salvage sale activities, resource support to timber and K-V reforestation, and TSI. Not included are general administration, timber management support to other resources, and road costs.

5. Roads are considered capital assets that have a cost and a value. Included are Forest Service appropriated-purchaser-credit, and purchaser-elected road construction and all engineering support expenditures.

Source: U.S. Forest Service Annual Report 1984.

percent by excluding the most uneconomic timber from sales, and federal revenues would actually have risen by at least US$40 million per year. (O'Toole, 1984)

In 1983 timber harvests could have been reduced by as much as 40 percent by excluding the most uneconomic timber from sales, and federal revenues would actually have risen by at least US$40 million per year.

Non-Timber Benefits and Below-Cost Timber Sales

The Forest Service has discounted attempts to devise incremental efficiency tests and instead emphasizes that timber operations must be evaluated as part of an overall management plan. It argues that timber harvests contribute to recreational access, control of fire, disease and insects, improvement of wildlife habitat, forage and fuelwood production, water management and community stability, and that these benefits more than offset losses on timber sales. Their argument is illustrated in Table II.G.4. The total benefits of cutting timber exceed direct costs in all regions. Remarkably, non-timber benefits range from around 36 percent of timber value in the Pacific and Southern states, where all analyses show timbering to be profitable, to 688 percent in the Alaskan region, where studies show timbering to be highly unprofitable.

There is considerably more irony in these data than in most government statistics: the Forest Service, under fire from environmentalists for its inattention to strict business principles, justifies its timber sales by their substantial recreational and environmental benefits. The supposed beneficiaries, including both environmental groups and fish and wildlife agencies in affected states, loudly oppose and are suing the Forest Service to stop it from providing the benefits they are allegedly receiving.

The debate between the Forest Service and environmental interests, centers on four issues. First, while the Forest Service assumes its road program will increase recreational benefits by improving access, opponents maintain that national forests already have enough roads to meet projected recreational needs. Second, the Forest Service claims its timber activities will benefit fish and wildlife and those who hunt or observe them, both by providing open browsing areas and by improving visitors' access. Opponents claim that the loss of undisturbed forests and tree-sheltered winter range will reduce the available habitat for many species, that stream siltation and changes in stream flow will impair fisheries, and that the road program will increase hunting pressure on remaining habitats. Third, the Forest Service suggests that timbering will raise water run-off and yields from many watersheds and increase the availability of water to downstream users. Opponents argue that soil erosion and increased sediment loading will decrease water quality and that the increase in seasonal variation in stream flows will impose additional costs on downstream users. Finally, the Forest Service argues that road construction associated with timber harvests lowers the costs of forest-protection activities and that below-cost salvage and rehabilitation harvests prevent the loss of valuable timber from pest infestation and fire. Opponents counter that the timber lost in mar-

The supposed beneficiaries, including both environmental groups and fish and wildlife agencies in affected states, loudly oppose and are suing the Forest Service to stop it from providing the benefits they are allegedly receiving.

ginal sites has no economic value and that if harvested at maturity, would actually result in economic losses. Moreover, they point out, fire protection costs are higher in areas accessible by roads because human visitors increase the risks of larger fires. The debate involves not just the magnitude of the non-timber values, but whether they are positive or negative.

Contributions to Community Stability

The Forest Service justifies its below-cost sales by arguing that the sales support local industry and help stabilize communities dependent on timbering activities. Yet, except in Idaho and Maine, logging and sawmilling employ less than one percent of the total labor force, and federal subsidies are no guarantee of job stability. Substantial shifts in employment have occurred in the industry in the last decade, resulting both from such broad economic factors as recession, high interest rates, an over-valued exchange rate that made Canadian imports cheap, and from the industry's relocation to the South. Furthermore, steady timber sales from national forests in periods of weak demand actually destabilize private logging industries.

Most payments from gross federal timber revenues go to communities that are comparatively well off. A state-by-state comparison of counties that received timber revenues with those that did not showed that recipient counties in the states where below-cost sales are chronic had above-average per capita incomes. In any case, since timber revenues are offset against payments to counties in lieu of property taxes on federal lands, reduced timber revenues would have no fiscal impacts on most counties outside the Pacific Northwest.

Fiscal Impacts

Timber operations cause significant economic losses. Rough conservative quantification of the magnitude of these losers, based on the accounts of the national forests that consistently lose money on timber operations, show that the total loss exceeded US$500 million for the six years, 1974–78 and 1982, or about US$85 million per year, excluding losses due to cross-subsidization.

A range of remedies is available to reduce below-cost sales. The narrowest option would impose a minimum bid restriction on timber sales to cover direct, separable production costs. A broader remedy would implement section 6(k) of the National Forest Management Act, in a way that removed more of the economically unsuitable areas from the timber base before forest management plans were developed. A still broader approach, one that deals with the underlying forces that promote uneconomic timber operations, would require two complementary changes. First, the budgetary weight of timber would need to be reduced by installing market-based user charges for a wider range of recreational and other services, retaining most of those revenues at the forest level. Second, the effective incentives of forest managers to respond to costs and returns would have to be strengthened by making each forest more self-sufficient financially, reducing their dependence on appropriated funds, and increasing the importance of retained net revenues in their total budgets.

Robert Repetto is Director, Program in Economics and Institutions at the World Resources Institute. Formerly, he was an associate professor of economics in the School of Public Health at Harvard University and a member of the economics faculty and the Center for Population Studies.

References

Advisory Commission on Intergovernmental Relations. 1978. *The Adequacy of Federal Compensation to Local Governments for Tax-Exempt Federal Land.* Washington, D.C., July.

Allen, Julia C. and Douglas F. Barnes. 1985. The Causes of Deforestation in Developing Countries. *Annals of the Association of American Geographers*, Vol. 75, No. 2, 1985:163–184.

Anderson, Dennis, and Robert Fishwick. *Fuelwood Consumption and Deforestation in Developing Countries.* World Bank Staff Working Papers No. 704, Washington, D.C., 1984.

Arnaud, Jean Claude and Gerard Sournia. "Les Forêt de Cote d'Ivoire, Une Richesse Naturrell en Voie de Désparision," *Les Cahier d'Outre Mer.*, 1980.

Ashton, Peter. "Aide Memoire on the State of Rain Forest Research and Its Application in Indonesia." Arnold Arboretum of Harvard University, Cambridge University: Massachusetts, July 20, 1984.

Asian Timber. "Logging Still Dominates Timber Industry in Sarawak." July/August, 1984.

Aufderheide, Pat and Bruce M. Rich. 1985. Debacle in the Amazon. *Defenders*, March/April.

Banco Central do Brasil. *Dados Estatísticos* (Brasilia), various years.

Barlow, Thomas, et al. 1980. *Giving Away the National Forest.* Washington, D.C.: Natural Resources Defense Council, June.

Bautista, Romeo, and John Power. 1979. *Industrial Promotion Policies in the Philippines.* Manila: Philippine Institute for Development Studies.

Berger, Richard. 1980. The Brazilian Fiscal Incentive Act's Influence on Reforestation Activity in São Paulo State. Ph.D. dissertation. Michigan State University, East Lansing.

Berthelsen, John. "Sabah Chief Inherits Troubled Economy," *Wall Street Journal*, June 5, 1985.

Beuter, John H. 1985. *Federal Timber Sales.* Washington, D.C.: Congressional Research Service, Library of Congress.

Bourke, I.J. 1986. International and Trade Barriers: The Case of Forest Products. Unpublished. Resources for the Future. March.

Breunig, E.F. 1985. Deforestation and Its Implications for the Rain Forests of South East Asia. In International Union for the Conservation of Nature, *The Future of Tropical Rain Forests in South East Asia.* Geneva.

Browder, John O. 1984. Tomando Conhecimento dos Importadores Norteamericanos de

Madeira Amazônica Brasileira. *Infoc Madeireiro*, Edicão Especial 3, (20). Brasilia: IBDF.

Browder, John O. 1985. Subsidies, Deforestation and the Forest Sector in the Brazilian Amazon. A Report to the World Resources Institute. Washington, D.C.

Brown, Lester, et al. 1985. *State of the World*. Worldwatch Institute. New York: W.W. Norton.

Bunker, Stephen G. 1980. Forces of Destruction in Amazonia. *Environment*, Vol. 20, No. 7, September: 14–43.

Bunker, Stephen G. 1985. *Underdeveloping the Amazon: Extraction, Unequal Exchange, and the Failure of the Modern State*. Urbana: University of Illinois Press.

Buschbacher, Robert J., Christopher Uhl, and E.A.S. Serrao. 1987. Large-Scale Development in Eastern Amazonia. In Carl F. Jordan, ed., *Amazonian Rain Forests: Ecosystem Disturbance and Recovery*. New York: Springer-Verlag.

Callahan, R.Z. and R.E. Buchman. "Some Perspectives of Forestry in the Philippines, Indonesia, Malaysia, and Thailand." Washington, D.C.: US Department of Agriculture, Forest Service, December 1981.

Choong, P.W. "Perspectives of LDCs on the Tropical Hardwood Sector." Paper presented to FAO/CTC Pacific Regional Workshop, Pattaya, 1980.

Contreras, Armando. 1982. Tropical Timber Processings in International Trade Development. FAO, Forestry Department Working Paper. Rome.

DBC Associates, Inc. *The Market for Softwood Lumber and Plywood in the People's Republic of China*. Paper prepared for the National Conference on Wood, January 15, 1983. Washing-ton, D.C.: National Forest Products Associations.

Dangdai Zhongguo de Linye [Contemporary China's Forestry]. Beijing: Zhongguo Shehui Kexue Yanjiu Yuan Chubanshe, 1985.

Das, K. "Dayaks Want Their Share of the Riches Now." *Far Eastern Economic Review*, December 2, 1977.

Department of Kehutan. *Draft Long Term Forestry Plan*. Jakarta, Indonesia, 1985.

———. *Statistik Kehutan Indonesia*. Jakarta, Indonesia, 1984.

Department of Statistics. *Angguran Hasil dan Perbalanjuan Bagi Tahun*, Various Issues, Kuala Lumpur, Malaysia.

Dowdle, Stephen. "Seeking Higher Yields from Fewer Fields," *Far Eastern Economic Review*, Vol 135, No. 12, 1987: 78–80.

Eckholm, Eric. 1976. *Losing Ground*. Worldwatch Institute. (New York: W.W. Norton) 1976.

Ehrlich, Paul R., and Anne H. Ehrlich. 1981. *Extinction: The Causes and Consequences of the Disappearance of Species*. New York: Random House.

FAO (A). "Tropical Forest Assessment Project," *Forest Resource of Tropical Asia*. Rome, 1981.

———(B). *Small and Medium Sawmills in Developing Countries*. Rome, 1981.

FAO. 1983. *Fuelwood Supplies in Developing Countries*. Rome.

———. *Tropical Forest Assessment Project*. Rome, 1986.

Fearnside, Philip M. 1982. Deforestation in the

Amazon Basin; How Fast Is It Occurring? *Intersciencia*, Vol. 72, No. 2: 82–88.

_____. "A Floresta Pode Acabar?" *Ciencia Hoje*, Vol. 2, No. 10, 1984, Janeiro/Fevereiro: 34–41.

_____. "The Causes of Deforestation in the Brazilian Amazon." Paper presented at the United Nations University International Conference of Climatic, Biotic and Human Interactions in the Humid Tropics: Vegetation and Climate Interactions in Amazonia. February 25–March 1. São Paulo: São Jose dos Campos, 1985.

Fitzgerald, Bruce. "An Analysis of Indonesian Trade Policies: Countertrade, Downstream Processing, Import Restrictions and the Deletion Program." CPD Discussion Paper #1986–22. Washington, D.C.: World Bank, 1986.

GAO. "Congress Needs Better Information on Forest Service's Below-Cost Timber Sales." Washington, D.C., June 1984.

Ghana Timber News. Vol. 7, No. 3, Accra, Ghana, 1979.

Gillis, Malcolm. "Fiscal and Financial Issues in Tropical Hardwood Concessions." Development Discussion Paper #110. Cambridge, Massachusetts: Harvard Institute for International Development.

Gillis, Malcolm, Ignatius Peprah and Michelline Mescher. "Foreign Investment in the Forest-Based Sector in Africa." Unpublished, Harvard University, Cambridge, Massachusetts.

Gillis, Malcolm and David Dapice. "External Adjustments and Growth: Indonesia." In *A Policy Manual for an OPEN Economy*. Edited by Rudiger Dornbusch. In press.

Goodland, Robert. 1985. Brazil's Environmental Progress in Amazonian Development. In

Change in the Amazon Basin: Man's Impact on Forests and Rivers, ed. John Hemming, pp. 5–35, Manchester: Manchester University Press.

Grainger, Alan. 1980. The State of the World's Tropical Forests. *The Ecologist*, Vol. 10, No. 1: 6–54.

Grainger, Alan. 1987. The Future of the Tropical Moist Forest. Unpublished paper. Washington, D.C.: Resources for the Future, May.

Gray, John W. 1983. *Forestry Revenue Systems in Developing Countries*. FAO, Forestry Paper No. 43. Rome.

Gregersen, Hans M. and Stephen E. McGauhey. 1985. *Improving Policies and Financing Mechanisms for Forestry Development*. Washington, D.C.: Inter-American Development Bank.

Guppy, Nicolas. 1984. Tropical Deforestation: A Global View. *Foreign Affairs*, Vol. 62, No. 4: 928–965.

Hartman, Richard. 1976. The Harvesting Decision When a Standing Forest Has Value. *Economic Inquiry*, Vol. XIV, No. 1:52–58

Hecht, Suzanna. 1985. Dynamics of Deforestation in the Amazon. Paper prepared for the World Resources Institute, November.

Hecht, Suzanna B. 1986. Development and Deforestation in the Amazon. Unpublished Report to the World Resources Institute, Washington, D.C., January.

Helfand, Gloria E. 1986. *Timber Economics and Other Resource Values: The Bighorn-Weitas Roadless Area, Idaho*. Washington, D.C.: The Wilderness Society.

Hunter, Lachian. "'Tropical Forests,' Plantations and Natural Stand Management: A Lesson from East Kalimantan," *Bulletin on*

Indonesian Economic Studies. 1984.

Hyde, William F. 1981. Timber Economics in the Rockies: Efficiency and Management Options. *Land Economics*, Vol. 57, No. 5: 630–637.

Hyde, William F., and John V. Krutilla. 1979. The Question of Development or Restricted Use of Alaska's Interior Forests, *The Annals of Regional Science*, Vol. 10, No. 1.

IBGE. *Anuario Estatistico*. Various Issues.

IBRD. *West Africa Forestry Sector Study*. Washington, D.C., 1976.

International Institute for Environment and Development and World Resources Institute. 1986. *World Resources 1986*. New York: Basic Books, Inc.

International Institute for Environment and Development and World Resources Institute. 1987. *World Resources 1987*. New York: Basic Books, Inc.

International Monetary Fund. 1983. *Interest Rate Policies in Developing Countries*. Occasional Paper No. 22. Washington, D.C., October.

Knowles, O.H. 1966. Relatorio ao Governo do Brasil Sobre a Producão e Mercado de Madeira na Amazônia. Projecto do fundo Especial No. 52. MI/SUDAM/FAO.

Krutilla, John, and Michael Bowes. In Press. *The Economics of Multiple Use Forestry*. ''Below Cost Timber Sales and Forest Planning.'' Baltimore, Maryland: Johns Hopkins University Press for Resources for the Future.

Lanly, Jean-Paul. 1982. *Tropical Forest Resources*. FAO, Forestry Paper No. 30. Rome.

Laarman, Jan G. *Government Incentives to Encourage Reforestation in the Private Sector of Panama*. Panama, USAID, September, 1983.

Leighton, Mark. ''The El Niño-Southern Oscillation Event in Southeast Asia: Effects of Drought and Fire in Tropical Forest in Eastern Borneo.'' Unpublished, Harvard University, Department of Anthropology, Cambridge, Massachusetts.

Leslie, A.J. 1987. A Second Look at the Economics of Natural Management Systems in Tropical Mixed Forests. *Unasylva*, 155 Vol. 39, No. 1: 46–58.

Li Kaixin. ''Concentrate Material Strength to Guarantee the Construction of Keypoint Projects,'' *Hongii [Red Flag],* September 1, 1983: 16–19.

Mackie, Cynthia. ''The Lessons Behind East Kalimantan Forest Fire,'' *Borneo Research Bulletin,* Vol. 16, No. 2: 67.

Matomoros, Alonso. 1982. *Papel de Incentivos Fiscales para Reforestación en Costa Rica,* Centro Agrónomico Tropical de Investigación y Enseñanza, Costa Rica, May.

Matthews, E. 1983. Global Vegetation and Land Use. *Journal of Climate and Applied Meteorology*, Vol. 22: 474–487.

Melillo, J.M., C.A. Palm, R.A. Houghton, and G.M. Woodwell. 1985. A Comparison of Two Recent Estimates of Disturbance in Tropical Forests. *Environmental Conservation*, Vol. 12, No. 1 Spring: 37–40.

Minckler, Leon. 1985. *Review of the Final Hoosier Forest Plan and EIS*. Eugene, Oregon: CHEC, Inc.

Moran, Emilio F. 1976. Agricultural Development in the Transamazon Highway. Latin American Studies Working Papers. Bloomington: University of Indiana.

Myers, Norman. 1980. *Conversion of Tropical Moist Forests*. Washington, D.C.: National Academy of Sciences.

Myers, Norman. 1984. *The Primary Source: Tropical Forests and Our Future*. New York: Norton.

Myers, Norman. 1985. Tropical Deforestation and Species Extinction: The Latest News. *Futures*, Vol. 17, No. 5, October 1985: 451–463.

National Research Council. 1982. *Ecological Aspects of Development in The Humid Tropics*. Washington, D.C.: National Academy Press.

Nor, Salleh Mohd. "Forestry in Malaysia," *Journal of Forestry*, March 1983.

Olson, J.S. 1975. Productivity of Forest Ecosystems. In National Research Council, *Productivity of World Ecosystems*. Washington, D.C.: National Academy Press.

O'Toole, Randal. 1984. Cross-Subsidization— The Hidden Subsidy. *Forest Planning*, May.

Page, John M. and Scott R. Pearson and Hayne E. Leland. "Capturing Rents from Ghanaian Timber," *Food Research Institute Studies*, Vol. 15, No. 1, 1976.

Page, John. "The Social Efficiency of the Timber Industries in Ghana," 1984.

Panyouto, Theodore. "Renewable Resource Management for Agriculture and Rural Development: Research and Policy Issues." Bangkok: ADC, November 1983.

Pearson, Scott and John M. Page. "Development Effects of Ghana's Forest Products Industry." Accra, Ghana: USAID, 1972.

Peprah, Ignatius. "Foreign Investment in Forest-Based Sector of Ghana." Unpublished, Harvard University, Cambridge, Massachusetts.

Pfeiffer. "Promotion of Marketing Trade and Value-Added." Addis-Ababa, Ethiopia: FAD, August 1980: 40–42.

Plumwood, Val, and Richard Routley. 1982. World Rainforest Destruction—The Social Factors. *The Ecologist*, Vol. 12, No. 1: 14–22.

Pompermayer, Malori Jose. "The State and the Frontier in Brazil: A Case Study of the Amazon." Ph.D. dissertation, Stanford University.

Porter, D. Gareth. 1987. Resources, Population and the Philippines' Future. Unpublished Report to World Resources Institute, Washington, D.C.

P.T. Data Consult. *A Comprehensive Report on the Indonesian Plywood Industry*. Jakarta, Indonesia, April 1, 1983.

Puyat, Jose, Jr. 1972. Prospects and Problems of the Wood Industries. In *Philippines Economy in the Seventies*, pp. 94–111. Quezon City, Philippines: Institute of Economic Development and Research, University of the Philippines.

Renmin Ribao [People's Daily]. Beijing, May 25, 1986.

Repetto, Robert. 1986. Soil Loss and Population Pressure on Java. *Ambio*, January/February.

Republic Gabon, Ministere des Eaux et Forêt. *La Forêt Gabonaise*. Libreville, Gabon, 1980.

Richards, Paul. 1973. The Tropical Rain Forest. *Scientific American*, Vol. 229, December: 58–67.

Ross, M.S. *The South-Sea Log Market in Relation to the Indonesian Transmigration Program*. Transmigration Area Development Project, Jakarta, East Kalimantan, Indonesia, 1982.

_____. "Forestry in Land Use Policy for Indonesia." Ph.D. dissertation, Oxford, University of Oxford, England, 1984.

Sample, V. Alaric, Jr. 1984. *Below-Timber Sales on the National Forests*. Washington, D.C.: The Wilderness Society, July.

Sarawak Study Group. *Logging in Sarawak: The Belaga Experience.* Petaling Java: Institute for Social Analysis.

Schaefer, Edward H. "The Conservation of Nature Under the T'ang Dynasty," *Journal of the Economic and Social History of the Orient,* Vol. 5, Part 3, December 1962: 279–308.

Scheuter, Ervin G., and J. Greg Jones. 1985. Below-Cost Timber Sales: Analysis of a Policy Issue. Ogden, Utah: USDA, Forest Service, Intermountain Research Station.

Schmithusen, Franz. "Forest Utilization Contracts: A Key Issue in Forest Policy." UNTC Pattaya Workshop on Tropical Hardwoods, Thailand, September 5, 1980.

Secrett, Charles. "The Environmental Impact of Transmigration," *The Ecologist,* Vol. 16, No. 2/3, 1986.

Segal, Jeffrey. "A Fragile Prosperity," *Far Eastern Economic Review,* April 14, 1983.

Setyono, Sastrosumarto, Herman Haerum, Atar Sibero and M.S. Ross. *A Review of Issues Affecting the Sustainable Development of Indonesia's Forest Land, Volume II.* Jakarta, Indonesia, November 30, 1985.

Simon, Julian and Herman Kahn, editors. *The Resourceful Earth.* New York: Basil Blackwell Inc., 1984.

Spears, John. 1979. Can the Wet Tropical Forest Survive? *Commonwealth Forestry Review,* Vol. 57, No. 3: 1–16.

Spears, John. 1983. *Sustainable Land Use and Strategy Options for Management and Conservation of the Moist Tropical Eco-Systems.* International Symposium on Tropical Afforestation, University of Waginengen, Netherlands, September.

_____(B). "The Role of Afforestation as a Sustainable Land Use and Strategy Option," *Let*

There be Forest. Agricultural University of Netherlands, 1983.

_____. "Key Forest Policy Issues for the Coming Decade in the Rain Forest Zone." Washington, D.C.: World Bank.

State Statistical Bureau. *Statistical Materials for China's Commodity Trade Prices, 1952–1983.* Beijing: Zhongguo Tongji Chubanshe, 1985.

_____. *State Statistical Yearbook 1985.* Beijing: Zhongguo Tongji Chubanshe, 1985.

_____. *State Statistical Yearbook 1986.* Beijing: Zhongguo Tongji Chubanshe, 1986.

SUDAM. "Incentivos Fiscais Liberados Pela SUDAM (Annualemente), Distribuição Setorial até o Mês de Setembro/83." SUDAM/DPO/DAI, 1983.

Sutlive, V.H., N. Altshuler and M.D. Zamura. *Where Have All the Forests Gone.* Williamsburg, Virginia: College of William and Mary, 1981.

Takeuchi, Kenji. *Mechanical Processing of Tropical Hardwoods in Developing Countries: The Asia Pacific Region.* World Bank Working Paper #1982–1. Washington, D.C., January 1982.

Tiing, Lau Buong. "The Effects of Shifting Cultivation on Sustained Yield Management in Sarawak's National Forests," *The Malaysian Forestor,* Vol. 42, No. 4, 1979.

Tucker, Richard and J. F. Richards, editors. 1983. *Global Deforestation and the 19th Century World Economy.* Durham, N.C.: Duke University Press.

USDA, Forest Service. 1985. *Analysis of Costs and Revenue in Four National Forests.* Washington, D.C.

USDA, Forest Service. 1986. *Timber Sale Program Information Reporting System: Draft Report to Congress.* Washington, D.C.

U.S. Congress, Office of Technology Assessment. 1984. *Technologies to Sustain Tropical Forest Resources.* Washington, D.C.

U.S. Congress, Office of Technology Assessment. 1987. *Technologies to Maintain Biological Diversity,* Washington, D.C.

Whitten, T.C. "Tropical Rain Forest of the Far East." Oxford, England: Clarendon Press, 1984.

Wilkinson, Charles F. and H. Michael Anderson. 1985. Land and Resource Planning in the National Forests. *Oregon Law Review,* Vol. 114, No. 1 and 2.

Wolf, Robert E., Assistant Division Chief, Environment and Natural Resources Policy Division. 1980. *State-by-State Estimate of Situations Where Timber will be Sold by the Forest Service at a Loss or a Profit.* Washington, D.C.: Congressional Research Service, Library of Congress, June.

World Bank. 1981. Brazil: Integrated Development of the Northwest Frontier. A World Bank Country Study, June 1981. Washington, D.C.

_____. *World Development Report.* Washington, D.C., 1985.

_____. *Ghana: Forestry Sector Review.* Washington, D.C., 1986.

World Resources Institute. 1985. Tropical Forests: A Call for Action. Report of a Task Force of WRI, World Bank, and the U.N. Development Programme. Washington, D.C.

World Resources Institute. *World Resources Report.* Washington, D.C., 1987.